# More Salad

# Two Raw Sisters

# More Salad

ALLEN&UNWIN
SYDNEY • MELBOURNE • AUCKLAND • LONDON

First published in 2024



Allen & Unwin
Level 2, 10 College Hill, Freemans Bay
Auckland 1011, New Zealand
Phone: (64 9) 377 3800
Email: auckland@allenandunwin.com
Web: www.allenandunwin.co.nz

83 Alexander Street
Crows Nest NSW 2065, Australia
Phone: (61 2) 8425 0100

A catalogue record for this book is available from the National Library of New Zealand.

ISBN 978 1 99100 635 6

Design by Katrina Duncan
Food stylist: Delivision
Clothing stylist: Kowtow
Special thanks to: Kate Hobbs Ceramics
Set in Area Normal
Printed and bound in China by 1010 Printing Co. Ltd
10 9 8 7 6 5 4 3

FSC www.fsc.org
MIX
Paper | Supporting responsible forestry
FSC® C016973

# Hello

**Welcome to our fifth cookbook, *More Salad***

At Two Raw Sisters, we love sharing recipes that make all eaters feel great. We're so excited to bring you another collection of our favourite salads – and if you know us, you'll know that our salads are anything but ordinary!

We hope this cookbook will inspire you to put fresh ingredients first, everyday. We'll show you how to cook them in fuss-free ways that are always delicious, creative and fun.

We encourage you to swap ingredients in and out depending on what's in your fridge, pantry and garden, saving you money and cutting down on waste.

We've also got loads of suggestions to help make the recipe suit your tastes. At the bottom of every recipe, you will find:

SWAP
Recommended simple swaps to get you started. These include swaps for vegetables, grains, nuts, seeds and dietary requirements. All recipes are adaptable and we encourage you to use them as a guideline.

TIP
Helpful time-savers, advice, and guidance on how you can make the most of each and every recipe.

DELICIOUS WITH
Recommendations to inspire pairing a salad with another salad and/or protein.

A quote we love is, *'Eat your food as your medicine, otherwise you have to eat medicine as your food.'* Neither of us are vegan or vegetarian, we simply love putting good ingredients first for this very reason. We believe that no matter your dietary requirements, financial situation, or age, all eaters should be able to make delicious salads and feel as great as we do every day.

If you use this cookbook, we promise you will never eat another bad salad in your life.

Enjoy!

Margo & Rosa x

# Swap with the Seasons

Our recipes are designed to be used as guides only, with ingredients swapped in and out according to the seasons. If you are cooking out of season or you don't have a specific vegetable a recipe calls for, simply swap it for a seasonal ingredient in the list over the page. Each recipe has a recommended swap to get you started. As you gain confidence with swapping ingredients in and out, we encourage you to get creative, using this guide to try other seasonal combinations.

# Summer

asparagus
beetroot
bok choy
broccoli
cabbage
capsicum
carrot
cauliflower
celery
cucumber
eggplant
fennel
green beans
kale
lettuce
mushroom
potato
rocket
spinach
sweetcorn
tomato
zucchini

---

# Autumn

beetroot
bok choy
broccoli
brussels sprouts
cabbage
capsicum
carrot
cauliflower
celery
cucumber
eggplant
fennel
kale
kumara
leek
lettuce
mushroom
parsnip
potato
pumpkin
rocket
silverbeet
spinach
sweetcorn
tomato
zucchini

# Winter

beetroot
bok choy
broccoli
brussels sprouts
cabbage
carrot
cauliflower
celery
cucumber
eggplant
fennel
kale
kumara
leek
lettuce
mushroom
parsnip
potato
silverbeet
spinach
yam

---

# Spring

asparagus
beetroot
bok choy
broccoli
cabbage
capsicum
carrot
cauliflower
celery
cucumber
eggplant
fennel
green beans
kale
kumara
leek
lettuce
mushroom
parsnip
potato
pumpkin
rocket
spinach
tomato
yam
zucchini

# Everyday Recipe Guide

For when you need fast inspiration . . .

## Super Speedy
## 15 minutes or under

### Raw / Fresh
Cos with Crispy Capers + Lemon
Chilli Cucumber + Avocado
Herby Quinoa + Halloumi
Almond Sesame Broccoli Slaw
Tomato, Cucumber, Feta + Smashed Olives
Cos, Avocado, Pickled Onion + Dijon Tahini
Zucchini + Garlic Paprika Almonds
Cabbage, Fennel, Celery Slaw + Preserved Lemon Oil

### Pan / Fry
Chilli Oil Fried Green Beans
Crunchy Lentils + Lemon Oil
Ginger Chilli Bok Choy
Asparagus + Lemon Walnut Crumble
Corn Cobs + Crispy Spring Onion Chilli Oil
Teriyaki Noodles + Garlic Fried Kale

### More / Dessert
Olive Oil Chocolate Mousse with Sea Salt
Mint + Lime Strawberries

## Quick + Easy
## 30 minutes or under

### Raw / Fresh
Ginger Peanut Black Rice
Lime, Coconut + Cashew Noodles
Tomatoes, Basil + Croutons

### Pan / Fry
Charred Cucumber, Bulgur + Almonds
Fried Chickpea + Herb Tabbouleh
Rice, Asparagus, Bok Choy + Lime Tamari Oil
Lemon Bulgur, Zucchini, Peas + Mint
Kimchi Fried Noodles
Bulgur, Caramelised Leeks, Cauliflower + Walnut
Brown Rice, Chilli, Corn + Avocado
Green Beans, Millet + Lemon Sumac Oil

### Oven / Roasted
Tahini Coated Cabbage + Pickled Onion
Kūmara, Creamy Kale + Smoky Tempeh
Cauliflower, Broccoli + Lemon Tahini
Fennel, Tomatoes, Chickpeas, Lemon + Herbs
Seedy Broccoli

## Quick + Easy 30 minutes or under ... continued

Eggplant + Avocado Whip
Turmeric Millet, Leeks + Garlic Miso Yoghurt
Roasted Cauliflower + Creamy Greens
Cheesy Crusted Pumpkin, Greens + Caper Oil
Harissa Carrots, Whipped Feta + Herb Carrot Top Oil
Garlic Thyme Pumpkin
Carrot Quinoa Tabbouleh
Cabbage, Yoghurt + Chilli Oil
Cauliflower, Tahini Garlic Yoghurt + Dukkah
Chilli Oil Mushrooms, Rice, Edamame + Cucumber
Pesto Brussels Sprouts + Feta

**More / Dessert**

Strawberry, Rhubarb + White Chocolate Crumble
Coffee Parfait, Salty Almonds + Chocolate
Peanut Mousse Pie

## Perfect for Work Lunches

**Raw / Fresh**

Herby Quinoa + Halloumi
Almond Sesame Broccoli Slaw
Ginger Peanut Black Rice
Lime, Coconut + Cashew Noodles

**Pan / Fry**

Charred Cucumber, Bulgur + Almonds
Crunchy Lentils + Lemon Oil
Fried Chickpea + Herb Tabbouleh
One Pan Zucchini, Couscous + Halloumi
Rice, Asparagus, Bok Choy + Lime Tamari Oil
Kimchi Fried Noodles
Zucchini, Green Beans + Pesto Barley
Bulgur, Caramelised Leeks, Cauliflower + Walnut
Brown Rice, Chilli, Corn + Avocado
Miso Barley, Mushrooms + Caramelised Onions
Green Beans, Millet + Lemon Sumac Oil
Teriyaki Noodles + Garlic Fried Kale

**Oven / Roasted**

One Tray Bake + Roasted Garlic Oil
Kūmara, Creamy Kale + Smoky Tempeh
Beets, Crispy Chickpeas + Dukkah Kale
Fennel, Tomatoes, Chickpeas, Lemon + Herbs
Eggplant, Rocket + Miso Yoghurt
Potatoes, Pumpkin, Carrots + Miso Sesame Oil

## Perfect for Work Lunches ... continued

Turmeric Millet, Leeks + Garlic Miso Yoghurt
Roasted Cauliflower + Creamy Greens
Cheesy Crusted Pumpkin, Greens + Caper Oil
Tomato Baked Cabbage + Smashed Olives
Miso Sesame Eggplant + Pumpkin Noodle Bowls
Beets, Pickled Onion, Avocado + Walnuts
Paprika Parsnips, Lentils + Herb Garlic Oil
Carrot Quinoa Tabbouleh
Rocket Pesto Pumpkin + Kale
Turmeric Satay Rice Bowls
Summer Vegetable One Tray Bake
Chilli Oil Mushrooms, Rice, Edamame + Cucumber
Mexican Beans, Charred Corn Salsa + Coriander Yoghurt

## Meal in Itself

**Raw / Fresh**
Herby Quinoa + Halloumi
Lime, Coconut + Cashew Noodles

**Pan / Fry**
Charred Cucumber, Bulgur + Almonds
Fried Chickpea + Herb Tabbouleh
One Pan Zucchini, Couscous + Halloumi
Rice, Asparagus, Bok Choy + Lime Tamari Oil
Kimchi Fried Noodles
Zucchini, Green Beans + Pesto Barley
Bulgur, Caramelised Leeks, Cauliflower + Walnut
Miso Barley, Mushrooms + Caramelised Onions
Teriyaki Noodles + Garlic Fried Kale

**Oven / Roasted**
Kūmara, Creamy Kale + Smoky Tempeh
Beets, Crispy Chickpeas + Dukkah Kale
Fennel, Tomatoes, Chickpeas, Lemon + Herbs
Eggplant, Rocket + Miso Yoghurt
Turmeric Millet, Leeks + Garlic Miso Yoghurt
Roasted Cauliflower + Creamy Greens
Tomato Baked Cabbage + Smashed Olives
Miso Sesame Eggplant + Pumpkin Noodle Bowls
Turmeric Satay Rice Bowls
Chilli Oil Mushrooms, Rice, Edamame + Cucumber
Mexican Beans, Charred Corn Salsa + Coriander Yoghurt

## Entertaining Showstoppers

### Raw / Fresh

Tomato, Cucumber, Feta + Smashed Olives
Cos, Avocado, Pickled Onion + Dijon Tahini
Lime, Coconut + Cashew Noodles
Tomatoes, Basil + Croutons

### Pan / Fry

Charred Cucumber, Bulgur + Almonds
Brown Rice, Chilli, Corn + Avocado
Miso Barley, Mushrooms + Caramelised Onions
Green Beans, Millet + Lemon Sumac Oil
Asparagus + Lemon Walnut Crumble
Corn Cobs + Crispy Spring Onion Chilli Oil

### Oven / Roasted

Tahini Coated Cabbage + Pickled Onion
One Tray Bake + Roasted Garlic Oil
Capsicum, Millet, Pesto + Rocket
Crispy Potatoes, Aioli + Smoked Paprika Seeds
Eggplant, Rocket + Miso Yoghurt
Eggplant + Avocado Whip
Creamy Leeks + Pine Nut Salsa
Eggplant, Grated Tomato + Basil
Roasted Cauliflower + Creamy Greens
Harissa Carrots, Whipped Feta + Herb Carrot Top Oil
Potatoes, Tomatoes + Basil Avocado
Cabbage, Yoghurt + Chilli Oil
Eggplant, Whipped Feta + Chimichurri
Cauliflower, Tahini Garlic Yoghurt + Dukkah
Summer Vegetable One Tray Bake

### More / Dessert

Sticky Date Puddings + Caramel Sauce
Strawberry, Rhubarb + White Chocolate Crumble
Olive Oil Chocolate Mousse with Sea Salt
Blueberry + Lemon Syrup Tray Cake
Raspberry Brownie Pudding
Coffee Parfait, Salty Almonds + Chocolate
Peanut Mousse Pie
Mint + Lime Strawberries
Hazelnut Caramel Slice

# Raw / Fresh

# Cos with Crispy Capers + Lemon

Feeds: 6
Time: 10 minutes

2 cos lettuces

**Crispy Caper Lemon Oil**

2 tablespoons cooking oil

4 tablespoons capers

peel stripped from 1 whole lemon (use a peeler)

½ teaspoon sea salt

4 tablespoons extra virgin olive oil

Heat the cooking oil in a frypan. Once the oil is hot, add the capers, lemon peel and salt. Fry until the lemon peel is golden brown around the edges and the capers are fried, stirring occasionally so nothing burns (8-10 minutes).

Spoon the lemon peel out and roughly chop into small pieces. Place in a small bowl. Add the fried capers and the cooking oil from the frypan, along with 2 tablespoons of the olive oil. Mix to combine.

To serve, arrange the cos lettuce leaves on a flat, round plate and drizzle the crispy caper lemon oil over. Top with the remaining 2 tablespoons of olive oil.

This is best eaten straight away.

---

### SWAP

Cos lettuce for rocket, spinach, iceberg lettuce or kale. In winter, sauté chopped silverbeet and mix through the crispy caper lemon oil for a warming green side.

### TIP

This crunchy fresh salad is perfect for barbecues, picnics or a weeknight meal. To make a heartier salad, add any canned legume or cooked grain and double the crispy caper lemon oil. Let the oil sit with the legume or grain, then toss with the lettuce just before serving. You could also top with crumbled feta or shaved parmesan.

### DELICIOUS WITH

Crispy Potatoes, Aioli + Smoked Paprika Seeds (page 126) and roast chicken.

# Chilli Cucumber + Avocado

Feeds: 4
Time: 10 minutes

- 1 cucumber, cut into bite-sized chunks
- 1 cup chopped coriander
- 1 avocado, cut into chunks
- 1 teaspoon sea salt

**Chilli Sesame Oil**

- 1 tablespoon chilli oil, homemade or store-bought
- 1 tablespoon sesame oil
- 1 tablespoon rice wine vinegar
- 1½ tablespoons tamari or soy sauce
- 2 garlic cloves, crushed and finely chopped
- 1 tablespoon sesame seeds

To a large bowl, add the cucumber, coriander, avocado and salt and set aside.

For the chilli sesame oil, mix all the ingredients together in a small bowl until well combined.

To serve, pour the chilli sesame oil over the cucumber and avocado chunks and gently toss.

This is best eaten straight away.

---

**SWAP**

Cucumber chunks for fresh tomatoes, grilled zucchini or asparagus.

**TIP**

If you don't like coriander, use any other herb. We love mint and/or parsley.

**DELICIOUS WITH**

Teriyaki Noodles + Garlic Fried Kale (page 104) and salmon.

# Herby Quinoa + Halloumi

Feeds: 4
Time: 15 minutes

¾ cup quinoa
1½ cups water

**Herb Yoghurt**

1 cup plain plant-based or dairy Greek yoghurt
1 cup chopped fresh herbs
zest and juice of 1 lemon
2 tablespoons extra virgin olive oil
2 garlic cloves, crushed
½ teaspoon sea salt

½ head broccoli, finely chopped
1 cup frozen green peas, blanched in boiling water for 5 minutes then drained
2 cups chopped fresh herbs
½ cup pumpkin seeds, toasted
2 tablespoons extra virgin olive oil
½ teaspoon sea salt

1 tablespoon cooking oil
250 g (9 oz) halloumi, cut into bite-sized cubes
1 avocado, cut into chunks

Add the quinoa and water to a pot. Bring the water to the boil and reduce to a simmer. Cook the quinoa uncovered for 7 minutes, then remove the pot from the heat.

For the herb yoghurt, process all the ingredients in a blender until you have a smooth, vibrant green sauce. (Alternatively you can use a stick blender.)

To a large bowl, add the cooked quinoa, broccoli, blanched peas, herbs, pumpkin seeds, olive oil and salt. Gently mix together.

Lastly, heat the cooking oil in a frypan and fry the halloumi cubes for 2-3 minutes on one side before flipping them over. Continue to cook for another 2-3 minutes until they are crispy and golden.

To serve, divide the quinoa between four bowls and top with the halloumi and avocado. Dollop the herb yoghurt on top.

This is best served straight away so the halloumi is gooey and soft.

Leftovers will keep in an airtight container in the fridge for up to 2 days. It is best to leave out the halloumi and avocado and add them fresh each time.

---

**SWAP**

Green peas for edamame beans. If you are dairy free, replace the halloumi with your favourite protein, such as chicken or prawns.

**TIP**

Don't throw away your broccoli stalk – grate it and add to everything else. If you are using a hand grater, hold the stem until you can't grate any more, then finely chop the rest.

**DELICIOUS WITH**

Zucchini + Garlic Paprika Almonds (page 52) and prawns.

# Almond Sesame Broccoli Slaw

Feeds: 8
Time: 15 minutes

- 1 head broccoli, cut into small pieces
- ¼ head green cabbage, very thinly sliced
- 1 cup edamame beans, blanched in boiling water for 5 minutes then drained
- ½ cup almonds, roasted and chopped
- 3 tablespoons sesame seeds
- 1 cup chopped coriander
- ½ teaspoon sea salt

**Almond Sesame Sauce**

- 2 tablespoons almond butter
- ¼ cup extra virgin olive oil
- juice of 1 lemon
- 2 teaspoons tamari or soy sauce
- 2 teaspoons sesame oil
- ½ teaspoon sea salt
- water to loosen

To a large bowl, add the broccoli, cabbage, edamame beans, almonds, sesame seeds, coriander and salt. Gently toss everything together.

For the almond sesame sauce, mix all the ingredients together in a small bowl until well combined. Loosen with water until you achieve a smooth consistency that easily runs off your spoon.

To serve, pour the sauce over the bowl of slaw and gently toss through.

Leftovers will keep in an airtight container in the fridge for up to 3 days.

---

**SWAP**

Almond butter for either tahini or peanut butter. Green cabbage for thinly sliced silverbeet, kale, spinach or red cabbage.

**TIP**

We like doing a half/half combination of broccoli and cauliflower. This recipe makes a lot – the leftovers are perfect for work lunches or weeknight dinners.

**DELICIOUS WITH**

Corn Cobs + Crispy Spring Onion Chilli Oil (page 102) and roast chicken.

# Tomato, Cucumber, Feta + Smashed Olives

Feeds: 4
Time: 15 minutes

**Pickled Red Onion**

½ red onion, very thinly sliced

1 tablespoon apple cider vinegar

¼ teaspoon sea salt

**Preserved Lemon Oil**

¼ preserved lemon, flesh and rind finely chopped

3 tablespoons extra virgin olive oil

1 garlic clove, crushed and finely chopped

200 g (7 oz) tomatoes, cut into bite-sized chunks

1 cucumber, cut into bite-sized chunks

½ cup olives, smashed with the back of a knife and pitted

100 g (3½ oz) feta, crumbled

1 cup chopped fresh herbs

For the pickled red onion, add the sliced red onion, apple cider vinegar and salt to a bowl. Toss to combine and allow the onion to pickle for at least 10 minutes.

To make the preserved lemon oil, mix the preserved lemon, olive oil and garlic together in a cup or small bowl.

To serve, place the tomato, cucumber, olives, feta, herbs and pickled onion in a bowl and pour the preserved lemon oil over. Gently toss to combine.

This is best eaten straight away.

---

**SWAP**

Feta for halloumi. If you don't like olives, use sun-dried tomatoes or capers.

**TIP**

If you don't have preserved lemons, use the zest and juice of 1 lemon. Double the pickled red onions and store in a jar in the fridge for up to 1 month. They make a delicious addition to any salad, sandwich, wrap or toast.

**DELICIOUS WITH**

Lemon Bulgur, Zucchini, Peas + Mint (page 80) and slow-cooked lamb.

TWO SAW SISTERS

# Ginger Peanut Black Rice

Feeds: 6-8
Time: 25 minutes

1 cup black rice
2½ cups water

**Ginger Peanut Sauce**

2 garlic cloves, crushed and finely chopped
1 tablespoon freshly grated ginger
4 tablespoons extra virgin olive oil
1½ tablespoons rice wine vinegar
3 tablespoons tamari or soy sauce
1 tablespoon peanut butter
3 teaspoons sesame oil
½ teaspoon chilli flakes or ½ fresh red chilli, finely chopped

1 cup edamame beans, blanched in boiling water for 5 minutes then drained
1 cucumber, cut into bite-sized chunks
1 cup chopped coriander
1 avocado, cut into chunks
¼ cup sesame seeds

Place the black rice and water in a pot. Bring to the boil, then reduce to a simmer and cook for 20-25 minutes. Once all the water has been absorbed, remove the pot from the heat and allow to cool.

For the ginger peanut sauce, mix all the ingredients together in a small bowl.

To serve, add the cooked black rice, edamame beans and cucumber to a large bowl. Drizzle the sauce over and gently toss everything together. Add the coriander, avocado and sesame seeds. Give the salad one final toss.

Leftovers will keep in an airtight container in the fridge for up to 3 days. If you want it to last, we recommend leaving out the coriander and avocado. Add them fresh each time.

---

**SWAP**

Black rice for brown rice or any other grain you have in the pantry.

**TIP**

Freezing root ginger in an airtight container makes it a lot easier to grate – no more stringy ginger!

**DELICIOUS WITH**

Ginger Chilli Bok Choy (page 84) and salmon, chicken or crispy tofu.

# Cos, Avocado, Pickled Onion + Dijon Tahini

Feeds: 4-6

Time: 15 minutes

**Pickled Red Onion**

1 red onion, finely diced
2 tablespoons apple cider vinegar
½ teaspoon sea salt

**Dijon Tahini**

2 tablespoons extra virgin olive oil
juice of 1 lemon
2 teaspoons hulled tahini
1 teaspoon Dijon mustard
½ teaspoon sea salt

2 heads cos lettuce
1 cup chopped fresh herbs
2 avocados, cut into quarters
½ cup seeds, toasted
100 g (3½ oz) feta, crumbled

For the pickled red onion, add the diced red onion, cider vinegar and salt to a bowl. Toss to combine and allow the onion to pickle for at least 10 minutes.

To a large bowl, add all the Dijon tahini ingredients and whisk together with a fork. Spoon about a third of the Dijon tahini into a separate small bowl to drizzle on top at the end.

Add the lettuce leaves and herbs to the large bowl and toss gently.

To assemble the salad, arrange half the lettuce on a flat, round plate, top with 4 avocado quarters, and sprinkle with half the seeds and feta. Then spoon over some of the pickled red onion. Repeat these layers. Lastly, drizzle the reserved Dijon tahini over the top.

Note: you won't need all the pickled red onion. The rest will keep in a jar in the fridge for up to 1 month.

This is best eaten straight away.

---

### SWAP

Pickled red onion for pickled cucumber, carrots or radishes. To supplement or replace the cos lettuce, use any other type of green that needs using up in the fridge or garden such as rocket, spinach, kale, silverbeet, cabbage and/or watercress.

### TIP

Any type of seed can be used in this salad, e.g. sunflower, pumpkin or sesame. If you are dairy free, leave out the feta.

### DELICIOUS WITH

One Tray Bake + Roasted Garlic Oil (page 114) and red meat, seafood or chicken.

# Lime, Coconut + Cashew Noodles

Feeds: 6
Time: 20 minutes

270 g (9½ oz) udon noodles

**Lime + Coconut Dressing**

½ cup coconut milk
zest and juice of 3 limes
2 teaspoons tamari or soy sauce
2 tablespoons freshly grated ginger
2 garlic cloves, crushed and finely chopped
2 teaspoons coconut sugar
2 teaspoons sesame oil
½ red chilli, finely diced
½ teaspoon sea salt

¼ head green cabbage, very thinly sliced
1 carrot, julienned
1 stalk of celery, thinly sliced
½ cup edamame beans, blanched in boiling water for 5 minutes then drained
2 cups chopped fresh herbs
½ cup cashews, roasted and chopped
½ cup shredded coconut, toasted

Cook the noodles according to the packet instructions.

For the lime + coconut dressing, mix all the ingredients together in a small bowl.

Add the cooked noodles, cabbage, carrot, celery, edamame beans, herbs, cashews and coconut to a large bowl. Pour half the lime + coconut dressing over and toss to combine.

To serve, transfer the noodles and vegetables to a salad bowl and drizzle the remaining lime + coconut dressing over the top.

Leftovers will keep in an airtight container in the fridge for up to 2 days.

---

**SWAP**

Any of the vegetables in this recipe for ones you have at home. We love thinly sliced raw bok choy, cucumber and spring onion. Refer to Swap with the Seasons (page 12) for more ideas. If you have no udon noodles, use whatever sort you do have – such as soba noodles, egg noodles or rice noodles.

**TIP**

This dressing is addictive. Make extra and drizzle over all your favourite green vegetables, or any vegetables you need to clear out of your fridge; toss it through a grain such as brown rice or quinoa; or use it as a dipping sauce for fresh rice paper rolls.

**DELICIOUS WITH**

Ginger Chilli Bok Choy (page 84) and seafood, chicken or tofu.

# Zucchini + Garlic Paprika Almonds

Feeds: 6
Time: 10 minutes

3 zucchini

**Garlic Paprika Almonds**

3 tablespoons cooking oil

½ cup almonds, roasted and chopped

zest and juice of 1 lemon

4 garlic cloves, crushed and finely chopped

2 teaspoons smoked paprika

½ teaspoon sea salt

1 tablespoon extra virgin olive oil

½ teaspoon sea salt

1 cup chopped fresh herbs

Using a potato peeler, shave the zucchini into thin ribbons and place them in a large bowl. Discard the core or see our tip on how to make great use of it.

For the garlic paprika almonds, heat the cooking oil in a frypan. Add the almonds, lemon zest and juice, garlic, smoked paprika and salt. Stir until the almonds are evenly coated, then cook for 3-5 minutes.

Pour the hot almonds, including the cooking oil, into the bowl of zucchini ribbons. Add the olive oil and salt. Toss everything together and allow to marinate for at least 10 minutes.

To serve, add the herbs to the zucchini ribbons and toss through. Arrange on a flat, round plate.

This is best eaten straight away.

---

### SWAP

Zucchini ribbons for cucumber ribbons.

### TIP

Chop the core of the zucchini into small pieces and freeze in an airtight container to use in smoothies. The addition of frozen zucchini creates a light, fluffy texture and is a great way to squeeze in (or hide) extra vegetables. These garlic paprika almonds are delicious on any salad, added to a cheese platter or enjoyed by the handful as a snack – we highly recommend making a big batch.

### DELICIOUS WITH

Harissa Carrots, Whipped Feta + Herb Carrot Top Oil (page 162) and red meat, chicken or white fish.

# Cabbage, Fennel, Celery Slaw + Preserved Lemon Oil

Feeds: 6
Time: 15 minutes

¼ cup green cabbage, very thinly sliced

1 fennel bulb, very thinly sliced

4 stalks celery, very thinly sliced

1 cup chopped fresh herbs

**Preserved Lemon Oil**

⅓ cup extra virgin olive oil

juice of 1 lemon

¼ preserved lemon, flesh and rind finely chopped

4 garlic cloves, crushed and finely chopped

1 teaspoon sumac powder

½ teaspoon sea salt

2 tablespoons dukkah

In a large bowl, toss together the cabbage, fennel, celery and herbs.

For the preserved lemon oil, mix all the ingredients together in a cup or small bowl.

To serve, pour the lemon oil over the slaw and sprinkle with the dukkah. Gently toss everything together.

Leftovers will keep in an airtight container in the fridge for up to 2 days.

---

**SWAP**

Green cabbage for thinly sliced cos lettuce, spinach, silverbeet or purple cabbage.

**TIP**

Sumac powder has a tangy, smoky, earthy and slightly sour flavour. You could use smoked paprika instead.

**DELICIOUS WITH**

Capsicum, Millet, Pesto + Rocket (page 118) with lamb, chicken or white fish.

# Tomatoes, Basil + Croutons

Feeds: 4-6
Time: 20 minutes

**Sourdough Croutons**

4 slices sourdough bread, cut into bite-sized chunks

3 tablespoons cooking oil

1 teaspoon sea salt

4–6 large tomatoes, cut into bite-sized chunks

3 tablespoons extra virgin olive oil

1 tablespoon balsamic vinegar

1 teaspoon sea salt

½ teaspoon freshly cracked black pepper

1 cup chopped basil leaves

1 cup rocket leaves

Preheat the oven to 190°C (375°F).

Toss the sourdough chunks with the cooking oil and salt on a baking tray. Bake for 15 minutes or until crispy.

To serve, toss together the tomatoes, olive oil, balsamic vinegar, salt and pepper in a large bowl. Add the croutons, basil and rocket and gently toss again.

Eat immediately.

---

**SWAP**

Tomatoes for watermelon, roasted stonefruit or charred zucchini.

**TIP**

We love adding feta, burrata (an Italian cheese made from mozzarella and cream) or crispy halloumi. If you are going to the trouble of making a batch of croutons, make twice as many and store half in an airtight container in the pantry for up to 5 days. An easy addition to any salad.

**DELICIOUS WITH**

Eggplant + Avocado Whip (page 138) and seafood, chicken, red meat or falafel.

# Pan / Fry

# Charred Cucumber, Bulgur + Almonds

Feeds: 4-6
Time: 30 minutes

1 cucumber, halved widthways then lengthways
2 tablespoons cooking oil
½ teaspoon sea salt

1 eggplant, cut into bite-sized chunks
3 tablespoons cooking oil
1 teaspoon sea salt

¾ cup bulgur wheat
boiling water

**Dijon Oil**

1 teaspoon Dijon mustard
¼ cup extra virgin olive oil
¼ preserved lemon, flesh and rind finely chopped
½ teaspoon sea salt

¼ cup olives, smashed with the back of a knife and pitted
½ cup almonds, roasted and chopped
¼ cup pumpkin seeds, toasted
1 cup chopped fresh herbs
3 tablespoons hulled tahini to drizzle over

Preheat the oven to 200°C (400°F).

To char the cucumber, put a frypan on a high heat. Coat the four cut cucumber pieces in cooking oil and salt and lay them in the hot pan. Cook on both sides (flat and round) for 2-3 minutes or until the skin is charred in spots. Remove from the heat and cut the cucumber into random bite-sized chunks.

Toss the eggplant with the cooking oil and salt on a baking tray. Roast for 25 minutes.

While the eggplant is cooking, add the bulgur wheat to a heatproof bowl and cover with boiling water. Cover the bowl with a plate or a clean tea towel and allow to sit for 20 minutes. The bulgur wheat will absorb all the water and expand. If you have any excess water once the 20 minutes is up, drain the bulgur wheat through a sieve.

For the Dijon oil, mix all the ingredients together in a cup or small bowl.

To serve, pour the Dijon oil onto the bulgur wheat and mix together with a fork. Tip into a large bowl and add the charred cucumber, eggplant, olives, almonds, pumpkin seeds and herbs. Gently toss to combine. Serve with a drizzle of tahini.

Leftovers will keep in an airtight container in the fridge for up to 3 days.

---

**SWAP**

If you are gluten free, swap bulgur wheat for millet, quinoa or brown rice.

**TIP**

Charring cucumbers enhances the flavour and will make you look at them in a whole new way.

**DELICIOUS WITH**

Rocket Pesto Pumpkin + Kale (page 178) and chicken, salmon or white fish.

# Chilli Oil Fried Green Beans

Feeds: 4
Time: 10 minutes

- 2 tablespoons chilli oil, homemade or store-bought
- 400 g (14 oz) fresh whole green beans, ends removed
- 1 teaspoon sea salt

Add the chilli oil to a wok or large frypan and place over a high heat. Once the oil is hot, add the beans and salt. Let the beans char for 2 minutes, then give them a stir and leave for another 2–3 minutes or until blistered and charred.

Leftovers will keep in an airtight container in the fridge for up to 3 days.

---

### SWAP

If green beans are not in season, use broccoli, zucchini or asparagus. Refer to Swap with the Seasons (page 12) for more ideas.

### TIP

If your chilli oil is super spicy, use 1 tablespoon chilli oil and 1 tablespoon cooking oil. If you want to use frozen green beans, defrost what you need in advance to get rid of any excess liquid, and then give them slightly longer in the pan at a higher temperature so they fry rather than steam.

### DELICIOUS WITH

Kimchi Fried Noodles (page 82) with seafood or chicken.

# Fried Chickpea + Herb Tabbouleh

Feeds: 4
Time: 25 minutes

¾ cup bulgur wheat
boiling water

2 tablespoons cooking oil
1 red onion, thinly sliced
400 g (14 oz) can chickpeas, drained and rinsed
3 garlic cloves, crushed and finely chopped
1 teaspoon sea salt
1 teaspoon ground cumin
1 teaspoon smoked paprika
¼ teaspoon ground cinnamon

100 g (3½ oz) cherry tomatoes, halved
¼ cucumber, cut into bite-sized chunks
1 head cos lettuce, sliced widthways
½ cup chopped parsley
½ cup chopped coriander
1 tablespoon extra virgin olive oil
½ teaspoon sea salt
4 tablespoons hulled tahini to drizzle over

In a heatproof bowl, cover the bulgur wheat with boiling water. Cover the bowl with a plate or a clean tea towel and allow to sit for 20 minutes. The bulgur wheat will absorb all the water and expand. If you have any excess water once the 20 minutes is up, drain the bulgur wheat through a sieve.

Heat the cooking oil in a frypan, then add the red onion. Cook for 10 minutes or until the onion is caramelised. Add the chickpeas, garlic, salt, cumin, smoked paprika and cinnamon. Cook for a further 5 minutes.

To serve, combine the bulgur wheat and the chickpea mixture in a large bowl. Add the cherry tomatoes, cucumber, cos lettuce, parsley and coriander. Drizzle the olive oil over and sprinkle with salt. Gently toss together. Serve with a generous drizzle of tahini.

Leftovers will keep in an airtight container in the fridge for up to 2 days.

---

### SWAP

Chickpeas for canned butter beans or cannellini beans. Swap lettuce for any other leafy green such as rocket, spinach, kale or silverbeet.

### TIP

We always use hulled tahini (rather than unhulled), as it is more pourable and less bitter because the outer layer of the sesame seeds has been removed.

### DELICIOUS WITH

Seedy Broccoli (page 132) and chicken, lamb or falafel.

# Crunchy Lentils + Lemon Oil

Feeds: 4-6
Time: 15 minutes

- 3 stalks kale, stalks discarded and leaves finely chopped

- peel stripped from 1 whole lemon (use a peeler)
- 4 spring onions, finely sliced
- 2 garlic cloves, crushed and finely chopped
- ⅓ cup extra virgin olive oil
- ¼ cup almonds, chopped
- ¼ cup pumpkin seeds
- juice of 1 lemon
- 1 teaspoon cumin seeds
- ½ teaspoon chilli flakes

- 400 g (14 oz) can brown lentils, drained and rinsed
- 150 g (5½ oz) feta, crumbled
- ½ cup olives, smashed with the back of a knife and pitted
- ½ cucumber, cut into bite-sized chunks
- 1 cup chopped fresh herbs

Add the chopped kale to a large bowl and set aside.

Heat a frypan and add the lemon peel strips, spring onion, garlic, olive oil, almonds and pumpkin seeds. Stir occasionally until the garlic starts to brown and the lemon peel starts to curl and toast. Add the lemon juice, cumin seeds and chilli flakes and cook for another minute or two, stirring frequently.

Pour the hot nut mixture, including all of the cooking oil, into the bowl of kale and toss well. Then add the lentils, feta, olives, cucumber and herbs. Gently toss everything together.

Transfer the salad to a flat, round plate.

Leftovers will keep in an airtight container in the fridge for up to 2 days.

---

### SWAP

Almonds and pumpkin seeds for whatever nuts and/or seeds you have in the pantry, such as walnuts, sunflower seeds and/or cashews. Swap kale out when you have heaps of silverbeet in the garden.

### TIP

You can use whatever herbs you have in abundance at the time – your favourite single herb or a combination of several. We love using a combination of parsley and coriander.

### DELICIOUS WITH

Carrot Quinoa Tabbouleh (page 172) and falafels, chicken or lamb.

# One Pan Zucchini, Couscous + Halloumi

Feeds: 4
Time: 35 minutes

**Chilli + Garlic Fried Zucchini**

2 tablespoons cooking oil

2 zucchini, cut into thin rounds

4 garlic cloves, crushed and finely chopped

½ teaspoon chilli flakes

½ teaspoon sea salt

**Couscous**

400 g (14 oz) canned or fresh tomatoes, cut in half

¾ cup pearl couscous

1½ cups vegetable stock

½ teaspoon sea salt

200 g (7 oz) halloumi, cut into bite-sized cubes

2 tablespoons extra virgin olive oil

4 cups rocket leaves

Select the grill function of your oven and preheat to 200°C (400°F).

Start by frying the zucchini. Heat the cooking oil in an ovenproof frypan. Once the oil is hot, add the zucchini, garlic, chilli flakes and salt. Stir-fry until the zucchini is half cooked. Tip the zucchini rounds into a bowl, including any oil, garlic and chilli.

To the same frypan, add the tomatoes, couscous, stock and salt. Bring to the boil and simmer uncovered for 12 minutes. Stir every couple of minutes to ensure the couscous doesn't stick to the bottom of the pan.

Once the couscous is cooked, add the semi-cooked zucchini and the halloumi. Mix together gently. Place the pan under the grill for 8–10 minutes.

This is best served hot, drizzled with olive oil and with rocket leaves on the side.

Leftovers will keep in an airtight container in the fridge for up to 3 days and can be reheated.

---

**SWAP**

When zucchini are out of season, we like to use mushrooms or broccoli. Refer to Swap with the Seasons (page 12) for more ideas.

**TIP**

Batch-cook tonight's dinner, storing the leftovers in an airtight container in the fridge to reheat and enjoy over the next 3 days. Cook once – eat multiple times. If you are gluten free, use millet or quinoa instead of couscous and reduce the stove-top cooking time to 7 minutes.

**DELICIOUS WITH**

Asparagus + Lemon Walnut Crumble (page 98) and seafood, such as salmon, white fish or prawns.

# Rice, Asparagus, Bok Choy + Lime Tamari Oil

Feeds: 6
Time: 30 minutes

¾ cup brown rice
2 cups water

2 tablespoons cooking oil
1 head broccoli, cut into florets
1 bunch asparagus spears, ends snapped off and remaining stems cut in half
½ teaspoon sea salt

**Lime Tamari Oil**
2 tablespoons extra virgin olive oil
2 tablespoons tamari or soy sauce
2 garlic cloves, crushed and finely chopped
juice of 1 lime
1 tablespoon freshly grated ginger
1 teaspoon sesame oil
½ teaspoon chilli flakes

1 avocado, cut into chunks
2 spring onions, finely sliced
1 bunch bok choy, finely sliced widthways
⅓ cup peanuts, roasted and chopped
½ cup chopped coriander

Put the brown rice and water in a pot and bring to the boil. Reduce to a simmer and cook for 20-25 minutes, or until all the water has been absorbed. Remove from the heat.

Heat the cooking oil in a large frypan and add the broccoli, asparagus and salt. Leave to char for 2-3 minutes. Give them a quick toss and leave to cook for another 2-3 minutes. Remove from the heat.

For the lime tamari oil, mix all the ingredients together in a cup or small bowl.

To serve, add the cooked rice, broccoli and asparagus, avocado, spring onion, bok choy, peanuts and coriander to a large bowl. Pour the lime tamari oil over and toss gently.

Leftovers will keep in an airtight container in the fridge for up to 3 days.

---

**SWAP**

When asparagus is out of season, use cucumber or refer to Swap with the Seasons (page 12) for more ideas.

**TIP**

The lime tamari oil is a delicious marinade for chicken or drizzled over salmon before baking in the oven. It also works well as a dipping sauce for spring rolls or dumplings. We highly recommend making a big batch. It will keep in a jar in the fridge for up to 2 weeks.

**DELICIOUS WITH**

Chicken, salmon, prawns or crispy tofu.

# Lemon Bulgur, Zucchini, Peas + Mint

Feeds: 6
Time: 25 minutes

1 cup bulgur wheat
boiling water

2 tablespoons cooking oil
2 zucchini, thinly sliced on a diagonal
½ teaspoon sea salt

**Garlic Thyme Oil**
4 garlic cloves, crushed and thinly sliced
leaves stripped off 4 stalks thyme
1 teaspoon cumin seeds
½ cup extra virgin olive oil

zest and juice of 1 lemon
½ cup almonds, roasted and chopped
1 cup frozen peas, blanched in boiling water for 5 minutes then drained
1 cup chopped mint leaves
1 cup chopped basil leaves
1 avocado, cut into chunks

In a heatproof bowl, cover the bulgur wheat with boiling water. Cover the bowl with either a plate or a clean tea towel and allow to sit for 20 minutes. The bulgur wheat will absorb all the water and expand. If you have any excess water once the 20 minutes is up, drain the bulgur wheat through a sieve.

Heat the cooking oil in a frypan. Once it's hot, add the zucchini and salt. Cook for 5 minutes, stirring every couple of minutes. When the zucchini has softened, remove the pan from the heat.

In a small frypan, cook the garlic, thyme, cumin seeds and olive oil over a low-medium heat for about 2 minutes, stirring every so often. As soon as the garlic starts to turn golden, immediately remove the pan from the heat and tip everything into a small bowl. You need to work quickly here – if the garlic burns, it turns bitter.

Allow the garlic thyme oil to infuse for at least 15 minutes for maximum flavour.

To serve, add the lemon zest and juice to the cooked bulgur wheat, along with the almonds, peas, mint, basil, avocado and zucchini. Pour over 4 tablespoons of the garlic thyme oil and gently toss everything together. Serve the remaining garlic thyme oil on the side to drizzle on top. (Garlic thyme oil will keep in a jar in the fridge for up to 1 month.)

Leftovers will keep in an airtight container in the fridge for up to 2 days.

---

**SWAP**

Zucchini for asparagus when in season or roasted eggplant chunks. Refer to Swap with the Seasons (page 12) for more seasonal ideas. Use plain extra virgin olive oil instead of the garlic thyme oil if you prefer or are pushed for time.

**TIP**

If you want to take a contribution to a barbecue or picnic and need a lovely summer salad that will survive the journey, this is the perfect choice. If you need to cater for people who are gluten free, replace the bulgur wheat with quinoa, millet or brown rice.

**DELICIOUS WITH**

Cauliflower, Broccoli + Lemon Tahini (page 122) and chicken, halloumi or seafood.

# Kimchi Fried Noodles

Feeds: 4
Time: 20 minutes

200 g (7 oz) udon noodles

2 tablespoons cooking oil
1 carrot, cut into semi-circles
1 head broccoli, cut into florets
2 spring onions, thinly sliced
3 garlic cloves, crushed and finely chopped
1½ cups kimchi
¾ cup edamame beans, blanched in boiling water for 5 minutes then drained

¼ cup sesame seeds
2 tablespoons sesame oil
4 tablespoons tamari or soy sauce

1 cup chopped coriander
2 tablespoons chilli oil or ½ red chilli, finely diced

Cook the udon noodles according to the packet instructions.

Heat the cooking oil in a large frypan. Once the oil is hot, add the carrot, broccoli and spring onion. Cook for 3 minutes, give them a toss and cook for another 3 minutes. Add the garlic, kimchi and edamame beans and cook for a further 2 minutes.

Add the cooked noodles, sesame seeds, sesame oil and tamari or soy sauce to the frypan and mix to combine. Cook everything together for 2 minutes.

Divide the kimchi fried noodles between bowls and top with the coriander and chilli oil or chilli.

Leftovers will keep in an airtight container in the fridge for up to 3 days.

---

### SWAP

Noodles for rice to turn this recipe into Kimchi Fried Rice.

### TIP

If you don't have kimchi in the fridge or don't like it, you can still make this recipe! Simply leave it out. Make a double portion and reheat for an easy work lunch or weeknight dinner.

### DELICIOUS WITH

Chilli Cucumber + Avocado (page 32) and salmon, prawns, chicken, tofu or a fried egg.

# Ginger Chilli Bok Choy

Feeds: 4
Time: 10 minutes

1 tablespoon cooking oil
2 tablespoons freshly grated ginger
4 garlic cloves, crushed and finely chopped
1 tablespoon tamari or soy sauce
1 teaspoon sesame oil
¼ red chilli, finely sliced
½ teaspoon sea salt

2 tablespoons cooking oil
2 heads bok choy, thinly sliced widthways

2 tablespoons sesame seeds

In a cup or small bowl, mix the cooking oil, ginger, garlic, tamari or soy sauce, sesame oil, chilli and salt.

Heat the cooking oil in a large frypan or wok and add the bok choy. Toss and cook for 2 minutes, then pour the sauce over and add the sesame seeds. Cook for another 2 minutes.

Tip onto a plate and serve while hot.

---

**SWAP**

Bok choy for green beans, asparagus or zucchini. Refer to Swap with the Seasons (page 12) for more ideas.

**TIP**

If you don't have fresh chilli, use ¼–1 teaspoon chilli flakes, depending on how hot you like it.

**DELICIOUS WITH**

Lime, Coconut + Cashew Noodles (page 50) and seafood or chicken.

# Zucchini, Green Beans + Pesto Barley

Feeds: 4-6
Time: 35 minutes

½ cup pearl barley
1½ cups water

2 tablespoons cooking oil
2 zucchini, cut into sticks
200 g (7 oz) fresh whole green beans, ends removed
½ teaspoon sea salt

**Pesto**

1 cup chopped fresh herbs
¼ cup walnuts, roasted
2 garlic cloves, crushed
3 tablespoons nutritional yeast
2 teaspoons apple cider vinegar
1 teaspoon sea salt
½ cup extra virgin olive oil

1 cup rocket leaves

Add the barley and water to a pot and bring to the boil. Turn the heat down to a low simmer, cover, and continue to cook until the barley is done – i.e. it is soft yet chewy. Start checking at 25–30 minutes, then every 5 minutes until the desired chewiness is reached. Add more water if the pot becomes dry before the barley is cooked; or if there is any excess water, drain it off. Using a fork, fluff up the barley to separate the grains.

Heat the cooking oil in a frypan and add the zucchini, beans and salt. Leave them to sit in the pan for a couple of minutes before giving them a toss and leaving them untouched for another 1–2 minutes. This allows them to become slightly charred. Once cooked, remove from the heat.

For the pesto, process all the ingredients in a blender until you have a vibrant green mixture. (Alternatively you can use a stick blender.)

To serve, toss the barley in a large bowl with about a quarter of the pesto. Add the zucchini and beans, the rocket and some more pesto. Toss gently. (If you don't end up using all the pesto, it will keep in a jar in the fridge for up to 1 month.)

Leftovers will keep in an airtight container in the fridge for up to 3 days.

---

**SWAP**

Pearl barley for another grain, such as brown rice, quinoa or millet.

**TIP**

You can roast the vegetables instead of pan-frying if you wish. Try using pumpkin, eggplant, kūmara, leeks and/or beetroot. Instead of chucking the bag of greens (spinach, rocket or watercress) that need using up in the compost, add them to the pesto.

**DELICIOUS WITH**

Cos, Avocado, Pickled Onion + Dijon Tahini (page 46) and seafood or chicken.

# Bulgur, Caramelised Leeks, Cauliflower + Walnut

Feeds: 6-8
Time: 25 minutes

½ cup bulgur wheat
boiling water

2 tablespoons cooking oil
2 leeks, thinly sliced into rounds
1 teaspoon sea salt
4 garlic cloves, crushed and finely chopped
4 strips of lemon peel (use a peeler)

**Dijon Tahini**

⅓ cup extra virgin olive oil
1 tablespoon hulled tahini
2 teaspoons Dijon mustard
juice of 1 lemon
½ teaspoon sea salt

½ cauliflower, florets very thinly sliced
2 cups chopped fresh herbs
½ cup walnuts, roasted and chopped

In a heatproof bowl, cover the bulgur wheat with boiling water. Cover with a plate or a clean tea towel and allow to sit for 20 minutes. The bulgur wheat will absorb all the water and expand. If you have any excess water once the 20 minutes is up, drain the bulgur wheat through a sieve.

Heat the cooking oil in a frypan. Add the leeks, salt, garlic and lemon peel. Cook for 5-8 minutes, or until the leeks become caramelised. Stir every so often to prevent the garlic from burning.

While the leeks are cooking, make the Dijon tahini. Mix all the ingredients together in a cup or small bowl.

To serve, tip the bulgur wheat into a large bowl. Add the leeks, raw cauliflower, herbs and walnuts, and then drizzle the Dijon tahini over. Give everything a toss.

Leftovers will keep in an airtight container in the fridge for up to 2 days.

---

**SWAP**

If you are gluten free, swap bulgur wheat for millet, brown rice or quinoa. In the Dijon Tahini, Dijon can be swapped for wholegrain mustard.

**TIP**

If you're not a fan of raw cauliflower, roast or fry the florets instead.

**DELICIOUS WITH**

Pesto Brussels Sprouts + Feta (page 192) and chicken, salmon or white fish.

# Brown Rice, Chilli, Corn + Avocado

Feeds: 6
Time: 30 minutes

1 cup brown rice
2 ½ cups water

2 cobs corn, cut in half
boiling water

1 avocado, cut into chunks
1 red chilli, finely chopped
1 cup chopped basil leaves
3 tablespoons extra virgin olive oil
zest and juice of 3 limes
1 teaspoon sea salt

Put the brown rice and water in a pot and bring to the boil. Reduce to a simmer and cook for 20–25 minutes, or until all the water has been absorbed. Remove from the heat.

Drop the corn cob halves into a large pot of boiling water and cook for 5 minutes. Immediately drain and rinse the corn with cold water.

To serve, place the slightly cooled brown rice in a bowl. Slice the corn kernels off the cobs with a sharp knife and add them to the rice. Add the rest of the ingredients and gently toss everything together.

Leftovers will keep in an airtight container in the fridge for up to 3 days. If you want to make it last, we recommend leaving out the avocado and basil and adding them fresh each day.

---

### SWAP

If corn is out of season refer to Swap with the Seasons (page 12) for other vegetable ideas. We love roasted broccoli, raw or roasted fennel bulb or charred cucumber. If you don't have brown rice, use any other grain you have in the pantry, such as black rice, quinoa or millet.

### TIP

In this recipe you can use frozen corn if fresh cobs are not available. Feel free to add any other frozen vegetables such as green peas, edamame beans or broad beans. Defrost the frozen vegetables you want to use by pouring boiling water over them in a heatproof bowl and leaving them for 5 minutes. Drain.

### DELICIOUS WITH

Cabbage, Yoghurt + Chilli Oil (page 174) and chicken or seafood.

# Miso Barley, Mushrooms + Caramelised Onions

Feeds: 6
Time: 45 minutes

1 cup barley
3½ cups water
1 tablespoon miso paste

2 tablespoons cooking oil
1 brown onion, thinly sliced
1 teaspoon sea salt
400 g (14 oz) mushrooms, sliced
4 garlic cloves, crushed and finely chopped
leaves stripped off 4 stalks thyme

2 tablespoons extra virgin olive oil
100 g (3½ oz) feta, crumbled
2 cups rocket leaves

Add the barley and water to a pot and bring to the boil. Turn the heat down to a low simmer, cover, and continue to cook until the barley is done – i.e. it is soft yet chewy. Start checking at 25-30 minutes, then every 5 minutes until the desired chewiness is reached. Add more water if the pot becomes dry before the barley is cooked; or if there is any excess water, drain it off. Using a fork, fluff up the barley to separate the grains. Stir the miso through.

Add the cooking oil, onion and salt to a frypan and fry for 10 minutes or until the onions have softened and caramelised. Add the mushrooms, garlic and thyme and cook for a further 5-8 minutes.

To serve, tip the cooked miso barley into a bowl and drizzle the olive oil over, mixing it through the grain to loosen it up. Add the mushrooms and caramelised onion and toss to combine. Lastly add the feta and rocket and mix gently.

Leftovers will keep in an airtight container in the fridge for up to 3 days.

---

### SWAP

Mushrooms for roasted pumpkin: roast pumpkin chunks with the brown onion, salt, garlic, thyme and cooking oil for 25-30 minutes at 200°C (400°F).

### TIP

Miso is a fermented soybean paste that is great for gut health. We love the brand Urban Hippie.

### DELICIOUS WITH

Seedy Broccoli (page 132) and red meat or chicken.

# Green Beans, Millet + Lemon Sumac Oil

Feeds: 6
Time: 20 minutes

¾ cup millet
1½ cups water

2 tablespoons cooking oil
400 g (14 oz) fresh whole green beans, ends removed
½ teaspoon sea salt

**Lemon Sumac Oil**
⅓ cup extra virgin olive oil
¼ preserved lemon, flesh and rind finely chopped
¼ cup chopped parsley
1 teaspoon sumac powder
juice of 1 lemon
1 teaspoon sea salt

1 cup chopped fresh herbs
½ cup almonds, roasted and chopped

Place the millet and water in a pot and bring to the boil. Reduce to a simmer and cook for 7 minutes. Remove the pot from the heat.

Heat the cooking oil in a frypan over a high heat. Add the beans and salt. Allow the beans to sit and cook for 2 minutes, then give them a toss and leave them for another 1–2 minutes. This allows them to become slightly charred. Remove the pan from the heat.

For the lemon sumac oil, mix all the ingredients together in a small bowl until well combined.

To serve, place the millet, beans and lemon sumac oil in a large mixing bowl. Add the herbs and almonds and toss everything together gently.

Leftovers will keep in the fridge in an airtight container for up to 3 days.

---

**SWAP**

Millet for any other grain you have in the pantry – we love using brown rice. Swap out beans for any other vegetable in season. Refer to Swap with the Seasons (page 12).

**TIP**

If you don't have preserved lemons, go and buy yourself a jar (or make some) because they're the best. Alternatively, use the zest and juice of 1 lemon.

**DELICIOUS WITH**

Summer Vegetable One Tray Bake (page 186) and white fish, salmon, chicken or halloumi.

# Asparagus + Lemon Walnut Crumble

Feeds: 6
Time: 10 minutes

2 tablespoons cooking oil
2 bunches asparagus spears, ends snapped off
½ teaspoon sea salt

**Lemon Walnut Crumble**

1 tablespoon cooking oil
¾ cup walnuts, roasted and chopped
2 garlic cloves, crushed and finely chopped
½ teaspoon sea salt
½ lemon, zest and juice

Preheat the oven to 200°C (400°F).

Heat the cooking oil in a frypan. When it's hot, add the asparagus and salt. Cook for 2 minutes, give it a toss, then cook for another 1-2 minutes. Once the asparagus is cooked but still has a bite to it, transfer it to a plate.

Using the same frypan, add the cooking oil, walnuts, garlic and salt. Cook, stirring frequently (being careful not to let them burn) until golden brown (about 3 minutes). Add the lemon zest and juice and cook for another 1-2 minutes, stirring frequently. Remove the pan from the heat.

To serve, top the asparagus with a generous portion of the walnut crumble.

This is best eaten straight away.

---

### SWAP

Walnuts for any nut or seed you have in the pantry. We love using pumpkin seeds or almonds. The walnut crumble can be served atop any other vegetable when asparagus is not in season. Refer to Swap with the Seasons (page 12).

### TIP

The asparagus season is short, so make use of the woody asparagus ends that otherwise would be thrown in the compost. Freeze them to use in future soups or vegetable stocks.

### DELICIOUS WITH

Herby Quinoa + Halloumi (page 36) and prawns, white fish or chicken.

# Corn Cobs + Crispy Spring Onion Chilli Oil

Feeds: 4
Time: 15 minutes

4 cobs corn, husks removed and each cob cut in half

water

**Crispy Spring Onion Chilli Oil**

2 tablespoons cooking oil

2 tablespoons chilli oil, homemade or store-bought

4 spring onions, thinly sliced

2 garlic cloves, crushed and thinly sliced

½ teaspoon sea salt

zest and juice of 1 lime

Bring a pot of water to the boil and add the corn halves. Boil for 3–5 minutes. Drain and set aside while you make the crispy spring onion chilli oil.

To a small frypan add the cooking oil, chilli oil, spring onion, garlic and salt. Fry over a medium heat until the spring onion and garlic start to get crispy. Keep a close eye on the garlic to ensure it doesn't burn. Once the garlic starts turning light brown, remove the frypan from the heat and add the lime zest and juice. Stir together.

To serve, arrange the corn cobs in a bowl or on a flat, round plate and spoon the crispy chilli spring onion oil over.

---

### SWAP

When corn isn't in season, swap for roasted zucchini halves or eggplant halves.

### TIP

The crispy spring onion chilli oil is so good and pairs well with anything. Double or triple the recipe and store in the fridge for up to 2 weeks.

### DELICIOUS WITH

Potatoes, Tomatoes + Basil Avocado (page 166) and red meat, chicken or fish.

# Teriyaki Noodles + Garlic Fried Kale

Feeds: 2
Time: 15 minutes

200 g (7 oz) udon noodles

**Teriyaki Sauce**

¼ cup tamari or soy sauce
1 tablespoon sesame oil
1 tablespoon freshly grated ginger

**Garlic Fried Kale**

1 tablespoon cooking oil
4 spring onions, thinly sliced
6 stalks kale, stalks discarded and leaves ripped into pieces
3 garlic cloves, crushed and finely chopped
½ teaspoon sea salt

¼ cup sesame seeds

Cook the udon noodles according to the packet instructions.

Make the teriyaki sauce by mixing the three ingredients together in a cup or small bowl.

For the garlic fried kale, add all the ingredients to a frypan and place over a high heat. Fry until the kale starts to char (5–8 minutes).

Add the cooked noodles, teriyaki sauce and sesame seeds to the kale and fry until the pan is dry, stirring constantly.

Leftovers will keep in an airtight container in the fridge for up to 2 days.

---

**SWAP**

Kale for bok choy, silverbeet or broccoli.

**TIP**

To make this dish gluten free, use rice noodles. The teriyaki sauce is addictive. Make extra and use it to marinate chicken, prawns, beef, venison, tofu or tempeh. Store in a jar in the fridge for up to 7 days.

**DELICIOUS WITH**

Chilli Oil Fried Green Beans (page 68) and salmon, prawns, tofu or chicken.

# Oven / Roasted

# Tahini Coated Cabbage + Pickled Onion

Feeds: 4
Time: 20 minutes

½ head green cabbage, cut into quarters
2 tablespoons cooking oil
1 teaspoon sea salt

**Pickled Red Onion**

1 red onion, very thinly sliced
2 tablespoons apple cider vinegar
½ teaspoon sea salt

**Miso Honey Tahini**

¼ cup hulled tahini
1 teaspoon miso paste
1 teaspoon honey
zest and juice of 1 lemon
½ teaspoon chilli flakes
¼ teaspoon sea salt
water to loosen

½ cup chopped fresh herbs
2 tablespoons sesame seeds
1 teaspoon sumac powder

Preheat the oven to 200°C (400°F).

Carefully transfer the cabbage quarters onto a baking tray. You want to keep them intact. Drizzle the cooking oil over and sprinkle with the salt. Gently rub over the cabbage. Place the tray in the oven to cook for 8–10 minutes. Turn the oven to the grill function and cook for a further 5 minutes or until the cabbage is becoming crispy and golden on the edges.

Meanwhile, pickle the red onion by pouring the apple cider vinegar over the slices and sprinkling with salt. Toss together and allow to sit for at least 10 minutes.

To make the miso honey tahini, mix all the ingredients together in a cup or small bowl. Loosen with water until you achieve a smooth, pourable consistency.

To serve, carefully arrange the cabbage quarters on a flat, round plate, keeping them intact. Drizzle the miso honey tahini over and arrange some pickled red onion on top. Lastly, sprinkle over the herbs, sesame seeds and sumac.

Leftovers will keep in an airtight container in the fridge for up to 2 days. Any leftover pickled red onion will keep in a jar in the fridge for up to 1 month.

---

**SWAP**

Green cabbage for purple cabbage.

**TIP**

If you don't have any lemons for the miso honey tahini or they are expensive, use 1 teaspoon apple cider vinegar instead.

**DELICIOUS WITH**

Fennel, Tomatoes, Chickpeas, Lemons + Herbs (page 130) with seafood, chicken or red meat.

# One Tray Bake + Roasted Garlic Oil

Feeds: 4-6

Time: 40 minutes

¼ pumpkin, preferably unpeeled, cut into bite-sized chunks
2 parsnips, cut into bite-sized chunks
1 kūmara, cut into bite-sized chunks
1 red onion, cut into thin wedges
2 garlic bulbs, top cut off to expose the cloves
leaves stripped off 4 stalks thyme
2 tablespoons cooking oil
1 teaspoon sea salt

¼ cup extra virgin olive oil
¼ teaspoon sea salt

Preheat the oven to 200°C (400°F).

Place the pumpkin, parsnip, kūmara, red onion, garlic bulbs and thyme on a large baking tray. Add the cooking oil and salt on top, toss carefully, and bake for 25 minutes. Turn the oven to the grill function and cook for a further 5-10 minutes. Remove from the oven.

Squeeze the softened garlic into a cup or small bowl and add the olive oil and salt. Mix with a spoon, mashing the garlic into a rough paste. Drizzle this garlic oil over the roasted vegetables and toss until well combined.

Serve in the baking tray or on a flat, round plate. Enjoy warm or at room temperature.

Leftovers will keep in an airtight container in the fridge for up to 4 days.

---

**SWAP**

Use any vegetables that are in season or need using from the fridge or garden. Refer to Swap with the Seasons (page 12) for more ideas.

**TIP**

Leave the skin on your pumpkin – it is delicious roasted! Our favourite pumpkin to use is buttercup (with the dark green skin). If you're going to the trouble of roasting a tray of vegetables, roast an extra trayful and enjoy for your lunch throughout the week. Prepping ahead and batch-cooking can make your life easier.

**DELICIOUS WITH**

Creamy Leeks + Pine Nut Salsa (page 144) and salmon, white fish, red meat or chicken.

# Capsicum, Millet, Pesto + Rocket

Feeds: 6
Time: 35 minutes

4 red capsicums, cut in half, core and seeds removed
8 garlic cloves, crushed with the back of a knife and skin removed
2 tablespoons cooking oil
½ teaspoon sea salt

½ cup millet
1 cup water
2 tablespoons extra virgin olive oil
½ teaspoon sea salt

**Pesto**
1 cup chopped fresh herbs
½ cup extra virgin olive oil
¼ cup sunflower seeds
1 teaspoon apple cider vinegar
½ teaspoon sea salt

2 cups rocket leaves
¼ cup pine nuts, toasted

Preheat the oven to 200°C (400°F).

Place the capsicum halves on a baking tray, skin side up. Tuck a garlic clove under each one to prevent the cloves burning. Drizzle the cooking oil over and sprinkle with the salt. Rub the oil over the capsicum (skin side) with your hands so they are evenly coated.

Roast for 25-30 minutes or until the capsicum halves are completely softened. Remove from the oven and set aside to cool before cutting the capsicum into random chunks. Place the garlic aside.

While the capsicums are roasting, add the millet and water to a pot and bring to the boil. Reduce to a simmer and cook for 7 minutes. Remove the pot from the heat and set aside. When it has cooled slightly, add the olive oil and salt and mix through with a fork.

For the pesto, process all the ingredients in a blender until you have a vibrant green mixture. (Alternatively you can use a stick blender.)

To assemble the salad, place half the rocket on a flat, round plate. Top this with half each of the millet, capsicum chunks, garlic, pesto and pine nuts. Repeat these layers.

Leftovers will keep in an airtight container in the fridge for up to 3 days.

---

**SWAP**

Red capsicums for eggplant, asparagus or zucchini. Refer to Swap with the Seasons (page 12) for more ideas.

**TIP**

We sometimes use sunflower seeds in our pesto as a cost-effective alternative to pine nuts. Pumpkin seeds also work well. Double the pesto recipe so you can have some left over to stir through pasta or a grain during the week. Add some roasted or stir-fried vegetables and animal or plant-based protein for a quick weeknight meal. Pesto also freezes well.

**DELICIOUS WITH**

Eggplant, Grated Tomato + Basil (page 146) and white fish.

# Kūmara, Creamy Kale + Smoky Tempeh

Feeds: 2
Time: 30 minutes

1 kūmara, cut into bite-sized chunks
1 tablespoon cooking oil
½ teaspoon sea salt

**Creamy Tahini**
2 tablespoons hulled tahini
1 tablespoon extra virgin olive oil
1 teaspoon sesame oil
1 teaspoon apple cider vinegar
½ teaspoon sea salt
water to loosen

4 stalks kale, stalks discarded and leaves ripped into pieces

**Smoky Tempeh**
2 tablespoons cooking oil
200 g (7 oz) tempeh, cut into bite-sized chunks
1½ teaspoons smoked paprika
2 tablespoons tamari or soy sauce

1 avocado, cut into chunks
¼ cup almonds, roasted and chopped

Preheat the oven to 200°C (400°F).

Toss the kūmara with the cooking oil and salt on a baking tray. Roast for 25 minutes.

While the kūmara is cooking, make the creamy tahini and smoky tempeh.

For the creamy tahini, mix all the ingredients in a cup or small bowl until smooth and creamy. You want a pourable consistency, so add water as necessary.

Place the ripped kale into a bowl and pour a third of the creamy tahini over it. Massage with your hands to tenderise the kale.

For the smoky tempeh, add the cooking oil to a frypan and place over a medium-high heat. Fry the tempeh until golden on both sides (5–10 minutes). Remove the pan from the heat and immediately add the smoked paprika and tamari or soy sauce. Stir gently until the tempeh is nicely coated and the pan is dry.

To assemble the salad, divide the creamy kale between two bowls and top with the roasted kūmara, smoky tempeh, avocado and almonds. Dollop the remaining creamy tahini on top.

Leftovers will keep in an airtight container in the fridge for up to 4 days.

---

**SWAP**

Tempeh for tofu or an animal protein such as salmon or chicken.

**TIP**

We make this a lot for our work lunches during the week. For one person, simply double the recipe for 4 days of lunches. Try adding extra vegetables to the kūmara before roasting. We love eggplant, carrots, fennel, broccoli and/or cauliflower.

**DELICIOUS WITH**

Smashed Polenta Brussels Sprouts (page 136).

# Cauliflower, Broccoli + Lemon Tahini

Feeds: 4
Time: 20 minutes

½ head cauliflower, cut into florets
½ head broccoli, cut into florets
4 spring onions, sliced into diagonal pieces
2 tablespoons cornflour
2 tablespoons cooking oil
½ teaspoon sea salt

**Lemon Tahini**
2 tablespoons hulled tahini
1 tablespoon apple cider vinegar
zest and juice of 1 lemon
½ teaspoon sea salt
water to loosen

¼ cup sesame seeds
½ teaspoon sumac powder
1 cup chopped coriander

Preheat the oven to 200°C (400°F).

Toss the cauliflower, broccoli and spring onion in a bowl with the cornflour, cooking oil and salt. Spread them out evenly on a baking tray and roast for 10 minutes. Turn the oven to the grill function and cook for a further 10 minutes.

For the lemon tahini, mix all the ingredients together in a cup or small bowl until smooth and creamy. Add just enough water to loosen it to a pourable yet still thick consistency.

To serve, add the sesame seeds and sumac powder to a large bowl and add the cauliflower, broccoli and spring onion. Drizzle the lemon tahini over and mix until everything is evenly coated. Add the coriander and give everything one final toss.

Leftovers will keep in an airtight container in the fridge for up to 3 days.

---

**SWAP**

Lemon tahini for our creamy greens dressing (page 151).

**TIP**

Tossing the vegetables in cornflour before cooking makes them go extra crispy. If you enjoy tofu, try coating it in cornflour before frying or baking in the oven.

**DELICIOUS WITH**

Paprika Parsnips, Lentils + Herb Garlic Oil (page 170) and red meat or salmon.

# Beets, Crispy Chickpeas + Dukkah Kale

Feeds: 6
Time: 35 minutes

- 3 large beetroot, cut into wedges
- 400 g (14 oz) can chickpeas, drained and rinsed
- 1 teaspoon ground cumin
- 2 tablespoons cooking oil
- 1 teaspoon sea salt

**Dukkah Kale**

- 5 stalks kale, stalks discarded and leaves ripped into pieces
- 3 tablespoons extra virgin olive oil
- 2 tablespoons dukkah
- ½ teaspoon sea salt

**Garlic Tahini**

- ¼ cup hulled tahini
- 4 garlic cloves, crushed and finely chopped
- 2 tablespoons extra virgin olive oil
- ¼ teaspoon sea salt
- water to loosen, if needed

- 1 avocado, sliced
- ½ cup walnuts, roasted and chopped
- 1 tablespoon dukkah

Preheat the oven to 200°C (400°F).

Place the beetroot, chickpeas, cumin, cooking oil and salt on a baking tray and toss to combine. Roast for 25-30 minutes.

For the dukkah kale, add all the ingredients to a bowl. Massage the kale with your hands until it is tender.

For the garlic tahini, mix all the ingredients together in a cup or small bowl. Add a little water if needed to create a pourable consistency.

To assemble the salad, place half the dukkah kale on a flat, round plate. Top with half the roasted beets and chickpeas, then half the avocado slices, walnuts, dukkah and a generous drizzle of garlic tahini. Repeat these layers.

Leftovers will last in an airtight container in the fridge for up to 4 days.

---

**SWAP**

Beetroot for cauliflower, leeks, pumpkin, fennel bulb or yams. Refer to Swap with the Seasons for more ideas (page 12).

**TIP**

A kale-based salad makes a great work lunch as it lasts up to 4 days. Simply leave out the avocado and add it fresh each time. To change up the flavour, swap the garlic tahini for aioli (page 127).

**DELICIOUS WITH**

Zucchini + Garlic Paprika Almonds (page 52) and red meat, chicken or salmon.

# Crispy Potatoes, Aioli + Smoked Paprika Seeds

Feeds: 6–8
Time: 75 minutes

8 medium potatoes, halved
water
½ teaspoon sea salt

**Aioli**

2 eggs
2 teaspoons Dijon or wholegrain mustard
½ teaspoon apple cider vinegar
¼ teaspoon sea salt
¾ cup olive oil

**Smoked Paprika Seeds**

½ cup pumpkin seeds
1 teaspoon cooking oil
1 teaspoon smoked paprika
½ teaspoon sea salt

3 tablespoons cooking oil
1 teaspoon sea salt

1 cup chopped fresh herbs

Preheat the oven to 200°C (400°F).

Add the potatoes to a pot, cover with water and add a good pinch of salt. Bring to the boil and reduce to a simmer for 20 minutes. Drain.

For the aioli, add the egg, mustard, apple cider vinegar and salt to a bowl. Beat with a hand-held whisk or stick mixer until it starts to fluff up and create bubbles (about 60 seconds). Add the olive oil in 6 individual pours, whisking for at least 30-45 seconds after each pour. Once your aioli has thickened, set it aside in the fridge.

For the smoked paprika seeds, place the pumpkin seeds in a dry frypan over a medium heat and toast until they start to pop. Add the cooking oil, smoked paprika and salt. Stir until the seeds are evenly coated and toast for a further 1-2 minutes.

Place the potatoes on a large baking tray. Using the bottom of a cup, press down each potato half to squash it a little. Drizzle with cooking oil and salt and roast for 45 minutes or until golden and crispy.

To serve, spread half of the aioli over the base of a flat, round plate, using the back of a spoon. Arrange the crispy potatoes on top. Spoon the remaining aioli over the potatoes and sprinkle with the smoked paprika seeds and herbs.

Leftovers will last in an airtight container in the fridge for up to 4 days.

---

### SWAP

Potatoes for kūmara, pumpkin or yams.

### TIP

Aioli is a staple of ours. Make a big batch and it will last up to 10 days in the fridge. The smoked paprika seeds are extremely addictive. Make a big batch and store in a jar for up to 2 weeks. Sprinkle them on top of salads and soups.

### DELICIOUS WITH

Cabbage, Fennel, Celery Slaw + Preserved Lemon Oil (page 54) or Cos with Crispy Capers + Lemon (page 30) and red meat, chicken, salmon or white fish.

# Fennel, Tomatoes, Chickpeas, Lemon + Herbs

Feeds: 6
Time: 25 minutes

- 2 bulbs fennel, cut widthways into 2 cm (¾ in) slices
- 200 g (7 oz) cherry tomatoes
- 400 g (14 oz) can chickpeas, rinsed and drained
- 1 teaspoon smoked paprika
- ½ teaspoon sea salt
- 2 tablespoons cooking oil

- ½ cup millet
- 1 cup water

- 1 cup chopped fresh herbs
- ¼ cup extra virgin olive oil
- juice of 1 lemon
- ½ preserved lemon, flesh and rind finely chopped
- ½ teaspoon sea salt

- 2 cups rocket leaves
- ½ cup olives, smashed with the back of a knife, pitted and chopped
- 2 tablespoons hulled tahini
- ½ cup walnuts, roasted and chopped

Preheat the oven to 200°C (400°F).

Place the fennel slices, cherry tomatoes and chickpeas on a baking tray. Sprinkle with the smoked paprika, salt and cooking oil and toss together. Roast for 10 minutes, then turn the oven to the grill function and cook for a further 5 minutes.

While the vegetables are cooking, place the millet and water in a pot and bring to the boil. Reduce to a simmer and cook for 7 minutes. Remove the pot from the heat.

Mix the herbs, olive oil, lemon juice, preserved lemon and salt together in a cup or small bowl.

Pour a quarter of this dressing over the millet and mix through with a fork. Reserve the remaining dressing for plating.

To assemble the salad, place half the rocket on a flat, round plate and top with half the millet, then half the roasted fennel, tomatoes and chickpeas. Add half each of the olives, the remaining dressing, tahini and walnuts. Repeat these layers.

Leftovers will keep in an airtight container in the fridge for up to 3 days.

---

**SWAP**

Fennel and cherry tomatoes for any other seasonal vegetables. Refer to Swap with the Seasons (page 12) for ideas. Millet is a tasty gluten-free grain but can be swapped out for another grain such as brown rice, couscous or quinoa.

**TIP**

To make the most of your fennel bulb, cut the stalks and leafy fronds into pieces and roast these with the bulbs. Alternatively, the fennel stalks can be added to soup and the fennel fronds can be chopped and used as a herb in salads or pestos.

**DELICIOUS WITH**

Cauliflower, Tahini Garlic Yoghurt + Dukkah (page 184) and salmon, white fish or chicken.

# Seedy Broccoli

Feeds: 4
Time: 25 minutes

**Seedy Oil**

⅓ cup sesame seeds
3 tablespoons dukkah
1 teaspoon sea salt
3 tablespoons cooking oil

1 large head broccoli, cut into florets
2 tablespoons hulled tahini to drizzle over

Preheat the oven to 200°C (400°F).

Mix the sesame seeds, dukkah, salt and cooking oil together in a small bowl.

Place the broccoli florets in a bowl and pour the seedy oil over. Toss to coat each floret.

Place the broccoli on a baking tray and top with any seedy oil left in the bottom of the bowl. Bake for 10 minutes, then turn the oven to the grill function and cook for a further 10 minutes.

To serve, arrange the roasted broccoli on a flat, round plate or in a bowl and drizzle with tahini.

Leftovers will last in an airtight container in the fridge for up to 2 days.

---

**SWAP**

Broccoli for cauliflower, parsnips, Brussels sprouts or carrots.

**TIP**

Don't throw away your broccoli stalk. Slice it lengthways into 1 cm (½ in) pieces and add to the bowl with the florets.

**DELICIOUS WITH**

Eggplant, Rocket + Miso Yoghurt (page 134) and chicken, salmon or white fish.

# Eggplant, Rocket + Miso Yoghurt

Feeds: 6
Time: 40 minutes

- 1 tablespoon miso paste
- 2 teaspoons sesame oil
- ¼ teaspoon sea salt
- 2 tablespoons cooking oil
- 2 eggplants, cut into bite-sized chunks

- ½ cup brown rice
- 1 ¼ cups water
- 2 tablespoons extra virgin olive oil
- ½ teaspoon sea salt

**Miso Yoghurt**

- ½ cup plain plant-based or dairy Greek yoghurt
- 2 tablespoons hulled tahini
- 2 teaspoons miso paste
- 2 teaspoons apple cider vinegar
- ¼ teaspoon sea salt
- water to loosen

- 3 cups rocket leaves
- ½ cup almonds, roasted and chopped
- ¼ cup dates, pitted and cut into quarters

Preheat the oven to 200°C (400°F).

Mix the miso, sesame oil, salt and cooking oil together in a large bowl. Add the eggplant chunks and mix until the eggplant is evenly coated. Place the coated eggplant chunks on a baking tray and roast for 25-30 minutes.

Put the brown rice and water in a pot and bring to the boil. Reduce to a simmer and cook for 20-25 minutes, or until all the water has been absorbed. Remove from the heat and toss the olive oil and sea salt through the rice. Set aside.

For the miso yoghurt, mix all the ingredients together in a cup or small bowl until you have a smooth creamy sauce. Add a little water to loosen it to a pourable yet still thick consistency.

To assemble the salad, place half the rocket on a flat round plate. Top with half each of the eggplant, brown rice, miso yoghurt, almonds and dates. Repeat these layers.

Leftovers will keep in an airtight container in the fridge for up to 3 days.

---

**SWAP**

Rocket for any leafy green you have, such as spinach, massaged kale, miners lettuce or a combination. If you want to keep things nut free, swap the almonds for pumpkin or sunflower seeds.

**TIP**

Change up the miso yoghurt for our creamy greens dressing (page 151).

**DELICIOUS WITH**

Beets, Pickled Onion, Avocado + Walnuts (page 160) and red meat, chicken, salmon or white fish.

# Smashed Polenta Brussels Sprouts

Feeds: 4
Time: 40 minutes

20 Brussels sprouts
water
½ cup polenta
1½ teaspoons sea salt
3 tablespoons cooking oil

**Preserved Lemon Tahini**

¼ cup extra virgin olive oil
2 tablespoons hulled tahini
juice of 1 lemon
¼ preserved lemon, flesh and rind finely chopped
2 cloves garlic, crushed and finely chopped
1 teaspoon sumac powder
½ teaspoon sea salt
water to loosen

Preheat the oven to 200°C (400°F).

Bring a pot of water to the boil. Add the Brussels sprouts and boil for 8 minutes. Drain. Lay them on a baking tray and smash each sprout a little by pressing down with the bottom of a cup. Carefully transfer them to a bowl and add the polenta, salt and cooking oil. Toss gently until the sprouts are evenly coated in polenta.

Place the coated Brussels sprouts on a baking tray and cook for 25 minutes or until golden and crispy.

While the Brussels sprouts are roasting, add all the preserved lemon tahini ingredients to a small bowl or cup. Mix until you have a smooth creamy sauce, adding water to loosen if needed.

To serve, place the Brussels sprouts on a flat, round plate and drizzle over 2-3 tablespoons of preserved lemon tahini. Serve the rest on the side.

Leftover Brussels sprouts will keep in an airtight container in the fridge for up to 3 days. Any leftover preserved lemon tahini will keep in a jar in the fridge for up to 2 weeks.

---

**SWAP**

Brussels sprouts for chunks of potato, kūmara or pumpkin. Cauliflower and broccoli florets are also delicious.

**TIP**

Add some nutritional yeast or grated parmesan to the polenta for a cheesy tang.

**DELICIOUS WITH**

Potatoes, Pumpkin, Carrots + Miso Sesame Oil (page 140) and red meat or chicken.

# Eggplant + Avocado Whip

Feeds: 4–6
Time: 30 minutes

2 eggplants, cut into bite-sized chunks
3 tablespoons cooking oil
1 teaspoon sea salt

**Avocado Whip**

1 avocado
1 cup chopped fresh herbs
¼ cup extra virgin olive oil
2 tablespoons hulled tahini
2 garlic cloves, crushed
juice of 1 lemon
½ teaspoon sea salt

100 g (3½ oz) feta, crumbled
¼ cup chopped fresh herbs
2 tablespoons dukkah
1 tablespoon extra virgin olive oil

Preheat the oven to 200°C (400°F).

Toss the eggplant chunks on a baking tray with the cooking oil and salt. Roast for 25-30 minutes.

While the eggplant is cooking, make the avocado whip. Process all the ingredients in a blender until smooth. (Alternatively you can use a stick blender.)

To assemble the salad, spoon all the avocado whip onto a flat, round plate. Use the back of a spoon to distribute it evenly around the plate. Arrange the eggplant chunks on top. Sprinkle over the feta, then the herbs and dukkah. Drizzle the olive oil over just before serving.

Leftovers will keep in an airtight container in the fridge for up to 2 days.

---

### SWAP

Eggplant for roasted spring carrots. In winter we love using pumpkin and/or yams. Refer to Swap with the Seasons for more ideas (page 12).

### TIP

You're going to love this avocado whip. Double the recipe so you can enjoy it as a dip for corn chips and/or crudités, on toast, or dolloped in tacos. Use whatever herbs you have on hand. We love using rocket and/or coriander.

### DELICIOUS WITH

Tomatoes, Basil + Croutons (page 58) and chicken or seafood.

# Potatoes, Pumpkin, Carrots + Miso Sesame Oil

Feeds: 6-8
Time: 40 minutes

5 baby potatoes, cut in half (or 2 medium-sized potatoes, cut into bite-sized chunks)

¼ pumpkin, preferably unpeeled, cut into bite-sized chunks

2 carrots, cut into bite-sized chunks

2 red onions, cut into thin wedges

leaves from 4 sprigs rosemary, chopped

2 tablespoons cooking oil

½ teaspoon sea salt

**Miso Sesame Oil**

2 tablespoons extra virgin olive oil

1 tablespoon miso paste

juice of 1 lemon

2 teaspoons sesame oil

2 teaspoons tamari or soy sauce

2 garlic cloves, crushed and finely chopped

½ teaspoon sea salt

400 g (14 oz) can lentils, drained and rinsed

1 cup rocket leaves

Preheat the oven to 200°C (400°F).

Place the potato, pumpkin, carrot, red onion and rosemary on a baking tray. Sprinkle the cooking oil and salt on top and toss to combine. Roast for 25 minutes. Give them another toss, then turn the oven to the grill function and cook for a further 5 minutes. Toss again, and grill for 3-5 minutes more. Once they are golden and starting to crisp up, remove from the oven.

While the vegetables are roasting, make the miso sesame oil by mixing all the ingredients together in a cup or small bowl.

To serve, add the lentils and rocket to the tray of vegetables, then drizzle the miso sesame oil over. Gently toss together.

Leftovers will keep in an airtight container in the fridge for up to 3 days. Any leftover miso sesame oil will keep in a jar in the fridge for up to 2 weeks.

---

**SWAP**

Refer to Swap with the Seasons (page 12) to utilise what's in abundance. Swap the lentils for any other canned legume you have at home – butter beans, chickpeas or cannellini beans.

**TIP**

If you have any vegetables that need using up, add them to the baking tray.

**DELICIOUS WITH**

Cos with Crispy Capers + Lemon (page 30) and red meat, chicken or salmon.

# Creamy Leeks + Pine Nut Salsa

Feeds: 4–8
Time: 35 minutes

- 2 leeks, halved widthways then lengthways
- 2 tablespoons cooking oil
- 1 teaspoon sea salt

**Lemon Yoghurt**

- ⅓ cup plain plant-based or dairy Greek yoghurt
- juice of 1 lemon
- ¼ teaspoon sea salt

**Pine Nut Salsa**

- ½ cup chopped fresh herbs
- zest of 1 lemon
- 2 tablespoons pine nuts, toasted
- 2 tablespoons extra virgin olive oil
- ½ teaspoon sea salt

Preheat the oven to 200°C (400°F).

Place the 8 cut leek pieces on a baking tray, cut side up, and drizzle with cooking oil and salt. Bake for 25-30 minutes until caramelised and soft.

Mix the yoghurt, lemon juice and salt together in a cup or small bowl.

For the pine nut salsa, mix all the ingredients together in another small bowl.

To serve, place the roasted leeks on a flat, round plate. Down each leek piece, drizzle some lemon yoghurt followed by a spoonful of pine nut salsa.

Leftovers will keep in an airtight container in the fridge for up to 2 days.

---

**SWAP**

In summer you can do this with zucchini halves or eggplant halves.

**TIP**

Pine nuts are expensive, so feel free to substitute whatever nuts or seeds you have in the pantry. Pumpkin seeds or walnuts work particularly well in this recipe.

**DELICIOUS WITH**

Roasted Cauliflower + Creamy Greens (page 150) and white fish, salmon or chicken.

# Eggplant, Grated Tomato + Basil

Feeds: 4
Time: 35 minutes

- 2 eggplants, cut in half lengthways
- 4 tablespoons cooking oil
- 1 teaspoon sea salt

**Grated Tomatoes**

- 3 tomatoes, grated
- 2 tablespoons extra virgin olive oil
- 1 teaspoon sea salt
- ½ teaspoon cracked black pepper

- 1 cup chopped basil leaves

Preheat the oven to 200°C (400°F).

Place the eggplant halves on a baking tray, cut side up, and drizzle over the cooking oil and salt. Bake for 30 minutes or until caramelised and soft.

While the eggplants are cooking, mix the grated tomatoes olive oil, salt and pepper in a bowl. If you have tomato skin remaining, roughly chop that up and add to the bowl.

To serve, arrange the eggplant halves face up on a flat, round plate. Top each with a generous dollop of grated tomatoes and a sprinkle of basil.

Leftovers will keep in an airtight container in the fridge for up to 1 day.

---

### SWAP

Eggplant halves for slices of sourdough bread.

### TIP

If you avoid cooking eggplant because you have had a bad experience with it, you have likely not added enough oil and salt before roasting in the oven, making it bland and rubbery. Eggplant is super absorbent so you need more oil than you think. And adding salt takes it to a whole new level flavour-wise. Give this recipe a go and discover how delicious eggplant can be.

### DELICIOUS WITH

Crunchy Lentils + Lemon Oil (page 72) and white fish, prawns or halloumi.

# Turmeric Millet, Leeks + Garlic Miso Yoghurt

Feeds: 6-8
Time: 30 minutes

2 leeks, sliced into rounds
2 parsnips, cut into sticks
400 g (14 oz) can butter beans, drained and rinsed
2 tablespoons cooking oil
2 teaspoons ground cumin
2 teaspoons ground turmeric
1 teaspoon sea salt

1 cup millet
½ teaspoon ground turmeric
2 cups water

**Garlic Miso Yoghurt**

1 cup plain plant-based or dairy Greek yoghurt
2 tablespoons hulled tahini
1 teaspoon apple cider vinegar
2 garlic cloves, crushed and finely chopped
1 teaspoon miso paste
½ teaspoon sea salt
water to loosen

6 stalks kale, stalks discarded and leaves finely chopped
1 cup almonds, roasted and chopped
2 tablespoons extra virgin olive oil

Preheat the oven to 200°C (400°F).

Place the leeks, parsnip and butter beans on a baking tray and toss with the cooking oil, cumin, turmeric and salt. Roast for 25-30 minutes.

While the vegetables are cooking, place the millet, turmeric and water in a pot and bring to the boil. Reduce to a simmer and cook for 7 minutes. Remove the pot from the heat.

For the garlic miso yoghurt, mix all the ingredients together in a bowl. Add a little water to loosen it to a pourable yet still thick consistency.

To assemble, place half the kale on a flat, round plate. Top with half each of the millet, roasted vegetables, garlic miso yoghurt, almonds and olive oil. Repeat these layers.

Leftovers will keep in an airtight container in the fridge for up to 4 days.

---

**SWAP**

Parsnip and leeks for summer produce such as asparagus, spring carrots and zucchini. Refer to Swap with the Seasons (page 12) for more ideas.

**TIP**

We choose to use canned legumes rather than soaking and cooking them ourselves, purely for convenience. There is little nutritional difference. Double the garlic miso yoghurt recipe and store the excess in a jar in the fridge for up to 7 days. Use it as a dressing on any other salad in this book. Preparing ahead makes your life easier.

**DELICIOUS WITH**

Chicken, salmon or red meat.

# Roasted Cauliflower + Creamy Greens

Feeds: 6
Time: 30 minutes

1 cauliflower

400 g (14 oz) can butter beans, drained and rinsed

1 teaspoon smoked paprika

1 teaspoon sea salt

2 tablespoons cooking oil

**Creamy Greens Dressing**

1 avocado

½ cup plain plant-based or dairy Greek yoghurt

1 cup chopped fresh herbs

zest and juice of 1 lemon

3 tablespoons extra virgin olive oil

1 teaspoon sea salt

3 stalks kale, stalks discarded and leaves finely chopped

½ head broccoli, cut into small pieces

½ cup almonds, roasted and chopped

1 avocado, cut into chunks

3 tablespoons extra virgin olive oil

Preheat the oven to 200°C (400°F).

Remove the leaves from the cauliflower. Discard the tough, stringy outer leaves and set aside the softer inner leaves. Cut the cauliflower into florets and place on a baking tray, along with the softer cauliflower leaves and butter beans. Sprinkle with the smoked paprika and salt. Toss with the cooking oil until the vegetables are evenly coated. Roast for 10 minutes, then turn the oven to the grill function and cook for a further 8-10 minutes.

While the cauliflower is cooking, make the creamy greens dressing. Process all the ingredients in a blender until you have a smooth creamy sauce. (Alternatively you can use a stick blender.)

In a large bowl, place the kale, broccoli and roasted cauliflower and butter beans. Gently toss to combine. Add the almonds, avocado and olive oil. Give it one final toss.

Arrange a third to half the salad on a flat, round plate. Dollop over the same proportion of the creamy greens dressing. Repeat these layers once or twice.

Leftovers will keep in an airtight container in the fridge for up to 3 days. If you want it to last, we recommend leaving out the avocado and adding it fresh each time.

---

**SWAP**

Avocado for 1 cup of blanched green peas or edamame beans. If you're not a big fan of kale, swap it out for any other leafy green such as cos lettuce, watercress, rocket or spinach.

**TIP**

Don't waste your cauliflower leaves – roast until golden, they're delicious! When we specify fresh herbs in a recipe, we encourage you to use whatever herb or herbs you love or have in the garden or fridge. Don't overthink it – use one or a combination of a few.

**DELICIOUS WITH**

Garlic Thyme Pumpkin (page 164) and chicken.

# Cheesy Crusted Pumpkin, Greens + Caper Oil

Feeds: 6
Time: 30 minutes

½ pumpkin, preferably unpeeled, cut into bite-sized chunks
2 tablespoons cooking oil
3 tablespoons nutritional yeast
1 tablespoons cornflour
1 teaspoon ground turmeric
½ teaspoon sea salt

2 tablespoons cooking oil
1 brown onion, thinly sliced
6 Brussels sprouts, thinly sliced lengthways
½ teaspoon sea salt

**Caper Oil**
2 tablespoons extra virgin olive oil
1 tablespoon wholegrain mustard
1 tablespoon capers, chopped
juice of 1 lemon
¼ teaspoon sea salt

4 stalks kale, stalks discarded and leaves finely chopped
½ cup walnuts, roasted and chopped
100 g (3½ oz) feta, crumbled

Preheat the oven to 200°C (400°F).

Toss the pumpkin, cooking oil, nutritional yeast, cornflour, turmeric and salt together and spread out on a baking tray. Roast for 25-30 minutes.

Meanwhile, heat the extra 2 tablespoons cooking oil in a frypan. Once the oil is hot, add the onion, Brussels sprouts and salt. Cook for 5-8 minutes, stirring every couple of minutes, until the vegetables begin to soften and turn golden brown.

For the caper oil, mix all the ingredients together in a cup or small bowl.

To serve, add the kale to a large bowl. Once the onion and Brussels sprouts have finished cooking, immediately tip them into the bowl. Pour the caper oil over and gently toss through. Add the cooked pumpkin (and any crispy crumbly bits), chopped walnuts and feta. Give everything a final toss.

Leftovers will keep in an airtight container in the fridge for up to 4 days.

---

### SWAP

Pumpkin for cabbage, fennel bulb, cauliflower or parsnips. Refer to Swap with the Seasons (page 12) for more ideas. If you don't have nutritional yeast, replace it with 3 tablespoons grated parmesan.

### TIP

Leftovers make a delicious lunch or dinner the next day. If you have any vegetables in the fridge or garden that need eating, such as potatoes, carrots or cauliflower, add them to the baking tray.

### DELICIOUS WITH

Tahini Coated Cabbage + Pickled Onion (page 112) and seafood, chicken or red meat.

# Tomato Baked Cabbage + Smashed Olives

Feeds: 4
Time: 35 minutes

2 tablespoons cooking oil
½ head green cabbage, cut into quarters
½ teaspoon sea salt

2 tablespoons cooking oil
1 brown onion, thinly sliced
2 garlic cloves, crushed and finely chopped
1 teaspoon ground cumin
1 teaspoon smoked paprika
½ teaspoon chilli flakes
½ teaspoon sea salt

400 g (14 oz) fresh or canned cherry tomatoes
400 g (14 oz) can chickpeas, drained and rinsed
¼ cup water
½ cup olives, smashed with the back of a knife and pitted
150 g (5½ oz) feta, crumbled

2 tablespoons extra virgin olive oil
½ teaspoon sea salt

Preheat the oven to 200°C (400°F).

Heat the cooking oil in a large ovenproof frypan (we used a skillet). Add the cabbage quarters and sprinkle each piece with salt. Sear one side of the cabbage quarters for 2–3 minutes, then flip and sear the other cut side for 2–3 minutes. Once the cabbage starts to soften and turn golden, remove from the pan to a plate.

To the same frypan, add the extra 2 tablespoons cooking oil. Cook the onion for 5 minutes or until soft. Add the garlic, cumin, smoked paprika, chilli flakes and salt and cook for another 2 minutes.

Add the cherry tomatoes, chickpeas, water and olives. Gently stir everything together, then nestle the cabbage wedges into the tomato sauce. Sprinkle with the feta. Place the frypan in the oven and cook for 10 minutes, then turn the oven to the grill function and cook for a further 5–10 minutes.

Remove from the oven, drizzle over the olive oil and sprinkle with salt. Serve while warm.

Leftovers will keep in an airtight container in the fridge for up to 3 days. This can easily be reheated in the oven.

---

**SWAP**

Cabbage quarters for zucchini halves or baked eggplant halves.

**TIP**

If you don't have all the spices, use different ones, for example curry powder, ground coriander or sumac powder. You can easily change up the flavour of this dish by using different spices.

**DELICIOUS WITH**

Brown rice, quinoa or millet and a drizzle of tahini. Add some prawns or white fish on the side.

# Miso Sesame Eggplant + Pumpkin Noodle Bowls

Feeds: 4
Time: 40 minutes

**Miso Eggplant + Pumpkin**

1 eggplant, cut into bite-sized chunks

¼ pumpkin, preferably unpeeled, cut into bite-sized chunks

3 tablespoons cooking oil

1 tablespoon miso paste

1 tablespoon sesame seeds

½ teaspoon sea salt

200 g (7 oz) udon noodles

**Ginger Miso**

2 tablespoons rice wine vinegar

2 tablespoons tamari or soy sauce

1 tablespoon miso paste

1 tablespoon freshly grated ginger

3 teaspoons sesame oil

1 teaspoon coconut sugar

zest and juice of 1 lime

1 tablespoon cooking oil

1 head broccoli, cut into florets

½ teaspoon sea salt

2 bunches bok choy, thinly sliced widthways

1 cup chopped coriander

1 cup cashews, roasted and chopped

½ red chilli, finely sliced

Preheat the oven to 200°C (400°F).

Spread out the eggplant and pumpkin on a baking tray.

Mix together the cooking oil, miso, sesame seeds and salt in a small bowl. Pour the mixture over the eggplant and pumpkin. Toss together until the sauce is evenly covering the vegetables. Bake for 25–30 minutes.

Meanwhile, cook the noodles according to the packet instructions.

For the ginger miso, mix all the ingredients together in a cup or small bowl.

To prepare the broccoli, heat the cooking oil in a wok or frypan. Once hot, add the broccoli and salt and cook for about 8 minutes, giving it a toss every 2 minutes.

To serve, divide the cooked noodles between 4 individual bowls and add the miso eggplant and pumpkin. Add the broccoli and raw bok choy. Top with coriander, cashews and chilli. Drizzle the ginger miso over.

Leftovers will keep in an airtight container in the fridge for up to 3 days.

---

**SWAP**

If you're gluten free, use rice noodles or soba noodles.

**TIP**

We love adding 2 tablespoons peanut butter or almond butter to the ginger miso to make a satay ginger miso. Think about doubling the ginger miso recipe and using it in other ways throughout the week. It is delicious poured over a side of salmon before baking it in the oven, or as a marinade for chicken or prawns before cooking them in a frypan or on the barbecue.

**DELICIOUS WITH**

Avocado, crispy tofu, salmon, chicken or prawns.

# Beets, Pickled Onion, Avocado + Walnuts

Feeds: 4-6
Time: 35 minutes

- 2 beetroot, cut into bite-sized chunks
- 3 parsnips, cut into bite-sized chunks
- 2 tablespoons cooking oil
- ½ teaspoon sea salt

**Pickled Red Onion**

- 1 red onion, thinly sliced
- 2 tablespoons apple cider vinegar
- ½ teaspoon sea salt

**Dijon Tahini**

- ¼ cup hulled tahini
- 1½ teaspoons Dijon or wholegrain mustard
- 1 teaspoon apple cider vinegar
- water to loosen

- 2 cups rocket leaves
- 1 avocado, cut into chunks
- ½ cup walnuts, roasted and chopped

Preheat the oven to 200°C (400°F).

Toss together the beetroot, parsnips, cooking oil and salt and spread out on a baking tray. Bake for 25 minutes.

For the pickled red onion, mix the thinly sliced onion, apple cider vinegar and salt in a bowl and leave to pickle for at least 10 minutes.

For the Dijon tahini, mix the tahini, mustard and apple cider vinegar in a cup or small bowl. Loosen with water if needed.

To assemble the salad, place half the rocket on a flat, round plate. Top with half each of the roasted beetroot and parsnip, avocado, pickled red onion, walnuts and a generous drizzle of Dijon tahini. Repeat these layers one more time.

Leftovers will keep in an airtight container for 4 days in the fridge. If you want it to last, we recommend leaving out the avocado and adding it fresh each time.

---

### SWAP

Omit the avocado if there is none available. Change up the vegetables depending on what is abundant or needs clearing out of the fridge. Refer to Swap with the Seasons (page 12) for ideas.

### TIP

We avoid cooking with olive oil, as it has a low smoking point. We use cold-pressed sunflower seed oil for cooking. Always avoid overcrowding your baking trays, spreading your vegetables over two trays if you feel it is a bit of a squeeze on one. Spreading them out means they cook evenly and turn golden and crispy. It also means you don't have to turn them at all during the cooking process.

### DELICIOUS WITH

Pesto Brussels Sprouts + Feta (page 192) and chicken or salmon.

# Harissa Carrots, Whipped Feta + Herb Carrot Top Oil

Feeds: 6
Time: 25 minutes

2 bunches spring carrots
400 g (14 oz) can chickpeas, drained and rinsed
2 tablespoons cooking oil
1½ tablespoons honey
1½ tablespoons harissa
1 teaspoon sea salt

**Whipped Feta**

50 g (2 oz) feta
¼ cup hulled tahini
¼ cup extra virgin olive oil
¼ cup water
zest and juice of 1 lemon
½ teaspoon sea salt

**Herb Carrot Top Oil**

1 cup chopped fresh herbs
1 cup chopped carrot tops
½ cup pine nuts, toasted
½ cup extra virgin olive oil
1 teaspoon chilli flakes
2 garlic cloves, crushed
½ teaspoon sea salt

2 tablespoons dukkah

Preheat the oven to 200°C (400°F).

Leave the small carrots whole and cut the larger ones in half lengthways. Place them on a baking tray with the chickpeas.

Mix the cooking oil, honey, harissa and salt together in a small bowl. Pour over the carrots and chickpeas and toss to combine. Bake for 15 minutes, then turn the oven to the grill function and cook for a further 8-10 minutes.

While the carrots are cooking, make the whipped feta. Process all the ingredients in a blender until you have a smooth creamy whip. Wash the blender. (Alternatively you can use a stick blender.)

For the herb carrot top oil, add everything to the blender and pulse until a green oil is formed. You still want some texture in it, rather than it being completely smooth.

To assemble the salad, evenly spread the whipped feta on the bottom of a flat, round plate, using the back of a spoon. Add the roasted carrots and chickpeas, followed by dollops of herb carrot top oil. Lastly, sprinkle over the dukkah.

Leftovers will keep in an airtight container in the fridge for up to 3 days.

---

### SWAP

Spring carrots for ordinary carrots. In which case, add extra herbs instead of the carrot tops in the oil. Swap the whipped feta for the avocado whip (page 139).

### TIP

The herb carrot top oil is a great excuse to use up fresh herb stems, such as coriander and basil. Avoid using any stems that are tough and stringy. If you don't use all of the oil here, it's great drizzled on roasted vegetables, fish or chicken. Turning the oven to the grill function is a great way to crisp up vegetables. If your roasted vegetables are cooked but not golden and crispy, put the tray under the grill for 5-10 minutes.

### DELICIOUS WITH

Green Beans, Millet + Lemon Sumac Oil (page 96) and white fish or chicken.

# Garlic Thyme Pumpkin

Feeds: 6
Time: 30 minutes

½ pumpkin, preferably unpeeled, cut into thin slices
2 tablespoons cooking oil
½ teaspoon sea salt

**Garlic Thyme Oil**

4 garlic cloves, crushed and thinly sliced
leaves stripped off 4 stalks thyme
1 teaspoon cumin seeds
½ cup extra virgin olive oil

½ cup chopped fresh herbs

Preheat the oven to 200°C (400°F).

Place the pumpkin slices on a baking tray and toss with the cooking oil and salt. Bake for 25-30 minutes.

While the pumpkin is cooking, make the garlic thyme oil. Cook the garlic, thyme, cumin seeds and olive oil in a small frypan over a low-medium heat, stirring every so often. When the garlic starts to turn golden (about 2 minutes), immediately remove the pan from the heat and tip the contents into a small bowl. You need to work quickly here – if garlic burns it turns bitter. Allow the garlic thyme oil to infuse for at least 15 minutes.

To serve, pour a generous amount of garlic thyme oil over the roasted pumpkin and toss gently. Add the chopped herbs and give it all one final gentle toss. (Any oil you don't use will keep in a jar for up to 1 month.)

Leftovers will keep in an airtight container in the fridge for up to 4 days.

---

**SWAP**

Pumpkin for green beans, asparagus, eggplant or cherry tomatoes. Refer to Swap with the Seasons (page 12) for more ideas. Thyme and pumpkin are a dream combination but rosemary also works well.

**TIP**

We love making a big batch of the garlic thyme oil and using it as a go-to dressing to elevate any dish. It also makes a delicious marinade for chicken, beef or lamb, or drizzled over a side of salmon before baking.

**DELICIOUS WITH**

Bulgur, Caramelised Leeks, Cauliflower + Walnut (page 90) and red meat, chicken, white fish or halloumi.

# Potatoes, Tomatoes + Basil Avocado

Feeds: 6
Time: 75 minutes

500 g (1 lb 2 oz) potatoes, cut in 2 cm (¾ in) slices
2 tablespoons cooking oil
1 teaspoon sea salt

6 tomatoes, cut in half widthways
1 tablespoon cooking oil
1 teaspoon sea salt

**Basil Avocado**
2 cups basil leaves
1 avocado
1 garlic clove, crushed
1 tablespoon extra virgin olive oil
1 teaspoon sea salt
juice of 2 lemons

1 cup chopped basil leaves

Preheat the oven to 200°C (400°F).

Toss the potatoes with the cooking oil and salt on a baking tray. Roast for 25–30 minutes.

On another baking tray, add the tomato halves. Drizzle over the cooking oil and sea salt. Place in the oven, under the potatoes. Once the potatoes have finished cooking, remove them from the oven. Move the tomatoes to the top and reduce temperature to 180°C (350°F). Continue cooking tomatoes for another 30–45 minutes.

For the basil avocado, process all the ingredients in a blender until you have a vibrant creamy green sauce. (Alternatively you can use a stick blender.)

To assemble the salad, spread two thirds of the basil avocado out over the base of a flat, round plate, using the back of a spoon. Arrange the roasted potatoes and tomatoes on top. Dollop the remaining basil avocado on top, and scatter with chopped basil.

Leftovers will keep in an airtight container in the fridge for up to 2 days.

---

### SWAP

When avocadoes are out of season, substitute for 1 cup of blanched green peas or edamame beans. Alternatively you can use aioli (page 127). If you don't have any basil you can use other herbs such as coriander, mint or parsley.

### TIP

If you are short on time you can use 200 g (7 oz) cherry tomatoes instead. After potatoes have been in the oven for 20 minutes, add the cherry tomatoes to the tray of potatoes and cook together for the last 10 minutes, or until the tomatoes start to blister.

### DELICIOUS WITH

Corn Cobs + Crispy Spring Onion Chilli Oil (page 102) and chicken, salmon or red meat.

# Paprika Parsnips, Lentils + Herb Garlic Oil

Feeds: 6
Time: 35 minutes

- 2 parsnips, cut into bite-sized chunks
- 1 red onion, cut into thin wedges
- 400 g (14 oz) can brown lentils, drained and rinsed
- 1½ teaspoons smoked paprika
- ½ teaspoon sea salt
- 2 tablespoons cooking oil

**Herb Garlic Oil**

- 1 cup chopped fresh herbs
- ½ cup extra virgin olive oil
- 1 garlic clove, crushed
- ½ teaspoon sea salt

- 6 Brussels sprouts, very thinly sliced
- 2 cups rocket
- 1 cup chopped fresh herbs
- ½ cup walnuts, roasted and chopped

Preheat the oven to 200°C (400°F).

To a baking tray, add the parsnip, red onion, lentils, smoked paprika and salt. Drizzle the cooking oil over and toss everything together. Bake for 20 minutes, then turn the oven to the grill function and cook for a further 5 minutes. This allows the lentils to turn nice and crispy.

Meanwhile, make the herb garlic oil. Process all the ingredients in a blender until you have a vibrant green oil. (Alternatively you can use a stick blender.)

Allow the tray of vegetables to cool slightly for 5 minutes. Then add the Brussels sprouts, rocket, herbs and walnuts. Drizzle the herb garlic oil over and toss gently.

Leftovers will keep in an airtight container in the fridge for up to 2 days.

---

### SWAP

Parsnip for fennel bulb, zucchini, beetroot or capsicums. Refer to Swap with the Seasons (page 12) for more ideas. Swap the rocket for any other leafy greens.

### TIP

Remember to not throw away your fresh herb stems (apart from ones that are woody and stringy). The herb garlic oil is a good way to use them up, along with the chopped herbs. They are packed with flavour.

### DELICIOUS WITH

Tomato, Cucumber, Feta + Smashed Olives (page 40) and chicken, seafood or red meat.

# Carrot Quinoa Tabbouleh

Feeds: 6
Time: 25 minutes

2 carrots, sliced thinly on a diagonal
2 tablespoons cooking oil
1 teaspoon honey
1 teaspoon cumin seeds
1 teaspoon smoked paprika
½ teaspoon sea salt

**Pickled Red Onion**
1 red onion, finely diced
2 tablespoons apple cider vinegar
½ teaspoon sea salt

¾ cup quinoa
1½ cups water

2 tablespoons extra virgin olive oil
juice of 1 lemon
¼ preserved lemon, flesh and rind finely chopped
1 cup chopped fresh herbs
¼ cup sesame seeds
2 tablespoons hulled tahini to drizzle over

Preheat the oven to 200°C (400°F).

In a bowl, toss together the carrot, cooking oil, honey, cumin seeds, smoked paprika and salt until the carrot slices are evenly coated. Pour the carrots onto a baking tray and bake for 10 minutes. Then turn oven to grill and cook for a further 5 minutes. Remove from the oven and allow to cool slightly.

For the pickled red onion, toss the diced red onion, apple cider vinegar and salt together in a bowl. Allow the onion to pickle for at least 10 minutes.

Add the quinoa and water to a pot. Bring the water to the boil, then reduce to a simmer. Cook the quinoa for 7 minutes. Remove the pot from the heat and set aside.

Add the cooked quinoa and carrots to a large bowl. Add the olive oil, lemon juice, preserved lemon, herbs and sesame seeds. Gently toss everything together.

To serve, arrange on a flat, round plate. Drizzle the tahini over and top with some pickled red onion.

Leftovers will keep in an airtight container in the fridge for up to 3 days. Any leftover pickled red onion will keep in a jar in the fridge for up to 1 month.

---

**SWAP**

Carrots for yams, pumpkin, eggplant, cauliflower, zucchini or beetroot. Refer to Swap with the Seasons (page 12) for more ideas.

**TIP**

Leave the skin on all your vegetables – including the pumpkin! There are a lot of beneficial nutrients in and just beneath the skin. Saves you time too!

**DELICIOUS WITH**

Eggplant, Whipped Feta + Chimichurri (page 176) and lamb or white fish.

# Cabbage, Yoghurt + Chilli Oil

Feeds: 6
Time: 20 minutes

- 1 green cabbage, cut into 2 cm (¾ in) slices
- 2 tablespoons cooking oil
- 1 teaspoon sea salt

**Lemon Yoghurt**

- ¾ cup plain plant-based or dairy Greek yoghurt
- 2 tablespoons extra virgin olive oil
- zest and juice of 1 lemon
- 2 garlic cloves, crushed and finely chopped
- ½ teaspoon sea salt

- ¼ cup chilli oil, homemade or store-bought
- 1 cup chopped fresh herbs

Preheat the oven to 220°C (425°F).

Arrange the cut cabbage on a baking tray. Drizzle the cooking oil over and sprinkle with the salt. Rub evenly over the cabbage.

Place in the oven and cook for 15 minutes, then turn the oven to the grill function and cook for a further for 3-5 minutes.

Mix all the lemon yoghurt ingredients together in a small bowl.

To serve, arrange the cabbage on a flat, round plate and dollop the lemon yoghurt over. Drizzle with chilli oil and sprinkle with herbs.

Leftovers will keep in an airtight container in the fridge for up to 3 days.

---

**SWAP**

Cabbage for zucchini, broccoli, cauliflower or eggplant. Refer to Swap with the Seasons (page 12) for more ideas.

**TIP**

Swap the lemon yoghurt for our garlic miso yoghurt (page 149).

**DELICIOUS WITH**

Rice, Asparagus, Bok Choy + Lime Tamari Oil (page 78) and seafood such as salmon, white fish or prawns.

# Eggplant, Whipped Feta + Chimichurri

Feeds: 4-6

Time: 35 minutes

2 eggplants, cut in half lengthways
4 tablespoons cooking oil
1 teaspoon sea salt
200 g (7 oz) cherry tomatoes

**Whipped Feta**

50 g (2 oz) feta, crumbled
¼ cup hulled tahini
¼ cup extra virgin olive oil
¼ cup water
zest and juice of 1 lemon
1 teaspoon sea salt

**Chimichurri**

1 cup chopped fresh herbs
½ cup extra virgin olive oil
½ red chilli, finely diced
zest and juice of 1 lemon
2 tablespoons red wine vinegar
4 garlic cloves, crushed and finely chopped
½ teaspoon ground cumin
1 teaspoon sea salt

2 tablespoons dukkah
3 tablespoons pine nuts, toasted

Preheat the oven to 200°C (400°F).

Place the eggplant halves face up on a baking tray. With a sharp knife, score the eggplant flesh of each half in 3 lines lengthways and evenly rub with the cooking oil and salt. Bake for 20 minutes. Add the whole cherry tomatoes to the baking tray and roast for another 10 minutes.

While the eggplant and tomatoes are roasting, make the whipped feta. Process all the ingredients in a blender until you have a smooth creamy whip. (Alternatively you can use a stick blender.)

For the chimichurri, mix all the ingredients together in a small bowl.

To assemble the salad, evenly spread the whipped feta over the base of a flat, round plate, using the back of a spoon. Arrange the roasted eggplant and tomatoes on top. Lastly, drizzle over some chimichurri and sprinkle with dukkah and pine nuts.

Leftovers will keep in an airtight container in the fridge for up to 2 days. Any leftover chimichurri will keep in an airtight container in the fridge for up to 4 days.

---

**SWAP**

Eggplant for asparagus. Refer to Swap with the Seasons (page 12) for more ideas.

**TIP**

Adjust the amount of chilli according to how hot you like your chimichurri. We personally love the extra heat of a whole red chilli! If you don't have a fresh red chilli, use ½ teaspoon chilli flakes. Leftover chimichurri is delicious drizzled over roasted vegetables, as a dressing in any salad, tossed through pasta, as a marinade for chicken or prawns, or spooned over a baked side of salmon.

**DELICIOUS WITH**

Cabbage, Fennel, Celery Slaw + Preserved Lemon Oil (page 54), falafels or slow-cooked lamb and flatbreads.

# Rocket Pesto Pumpkin + Kale

Feeds: 4-6
Time: 35 minutes

½ pumpkin, preferably unpeeled, cut into bite-sized chunks
2 tablespoons cooking oil
½ teaspoon sea salt
3 spring onions, white part thinly sliced and green part put aside for serving

**Rocket Pesto**

1 cup rocket leaves
1 cup chopped fresh herbs
¼ cup pine nuts or chopped walnuts
2 tablespoons nutritional yeast
zest and juice of 1 lemon
1 teaspoon sea salt
⅓ cup extra virgin olive oil

6 stalks kale, stalks discarded and leaves finely chopped
green tops of 3 spring onions, thinly sliced
½ cup pumpkin seeds, toasted

Preheat the oven to 200°C (400°F).

Place the pumpkin on a baking tray and toss with the cooking oil and salt. Bake for 20 minutes. Once the 20 minutes is up, sprinkle the thinly sliced spring onion whites on top and cook for a further 10 minutes.

Meanwhile, make the rocket pesto by processing all the ingredients in a blender. We prefer to have the pesto slightly chunky, but if you like a smoother texture just blend it for longer.

To a bowl, add the chopped kale, spring onion greens and pumpkin seeds. Then add the roasted pumpkin and spring onion, along with 4 generous dollops of rocket pesto. Gently toss together.

Leftovers will keep in an airtight container in the fridge for up to 3 days. Any leftover pesto will keep in a jar in the fridge for up to 1 month.

---

**SWAP**

Pumpkin for potatoes, Brussels sprouts, kūmara or cauliflower. Refer to Swap with the Seasons (page 12) for more ideas. You can also swap the nutritional yeast in the rocket pesto for grated parmesan.

**TIP**

You could add a grain such as brown rice, millet or quinoa and/or a can of legumes to this salad as a cost-effective way of adding protein and making it go further. Any leftovers make a great quick weeknight meal or work lunch.

**DELICIOUS WITH**

Charred Cucumber, Bulgur + Almonds (page 66) and chicken or red meat.

# Turmeric Satay Rice Bowls

Feeds: 2
Time: 35 minutes

½ cup brown rice
1 ¼ cups water

1 eggplant, cut into bite-sized chunks
¼ green cabbage, cut into large pieces
3 tablespoons cooking oil
1 teaspoon sea salt

**Turmeric Satay**

2 tablespoons peanut butter
2 tablespoons tamari or soy sauce
1 tablespoon freshly grated ginger
1 garlic clove, crushed and finely chopped
1 teaspoon sesame oil
1 teaspoon ground turmeric
1 teaspoon apple cider vinegar
½ teaspoon sea salt
water to loosen

1 avocado, cut into chunks
¼ cup chopped fresh herbs
¼ cup peanuts, roasted and chopped

Preheat the oven to 200°C (400°F).

Put the brown rice and water in a pot and bring to the boil. Reduce to a simmer and cook for 20-25 minutes, or until all the water has been absorbed. Remove from the heat.

Place the eggplant, cabbage, cooking oil and salt on a baking tray and toss together. Bake for 15 minutes. Then remove the cabbage and put the eggplant back in the oven for a further 5-10 minutes or until soft and golden.

While the brown rice and vegetables are cooking, make the turmeric satay. Mix all the ingredients together in a cup or small bowl until smooth and creamy. You want a pourable consistency so add a little more water if you need to.

To serve, mix a third of the turmeric satay through the cooked brown rice. Divide the brown rice between two individual bowls. Add the roasted eggplant and cabbage, followed by the avocado, herbs, peanuts and the rest of the turmeric satay.

Leftovers will keep in an airtight container in the fridge for up to 3 days. We recommend leaving out the avocado and adding it fresh each time.

---

### SWAP

When eggplants are expensive we love using broccoli instead. Refer to Swap with the Seasons (page 12) for more ideas.

### TIP

We highly recommend doubling the turmeric satay recipe and storing the excess in a jar in the fridge to use in other ways throughout the week.
It is delicious tossed through noodles and served alongside a range of different raw and/or cooked vegetables in a bowl. Add in some chicken, prawns, salmon or tofu and you have yourself a tasty turmeric satay noodle bowl.

### DELICIOUS WITH

Tofu, salmon, prawns or chicken.

# Cauliflower, Tahini Garlic Yoghurt + Dukkah

Feeds: 4-6
Time: 30 minutes

1 cauliflower, cut into florets
¼ teaspoon ground cinnamon
1 teaspoon smoked paprika
1 teaspoon ground cumin
2 tablespoons cooking oil
1 teaspoon sea salt

**Tahini Garlic Yoghurt**
½ cup plain plant-based or dairy Greek yoghurt
¼ cup hulled tahini
1 tablespoon extra virgin olive oil
zest and juice of 1 lemon
1 garlic clove, crushed and chopped
½ teaspoon sea salt
water to loosen

1 cup chopped fresh herbs
¼ cup almonds, roasted and chopped
¼ cup dukkah
2 tablespoons extra virgin olive oil

Preheat the oven to 200°C (400°F).

Place the cauliflower on a baking tray. Toss with the cinnamon, smoked paprika, cumin, cooking oil and salt until the cauliflower is evenly coated. Bake for 20-25 minutes.

Meanwhile, make the tahini garlic yoghurt by mixing all the ingredients together in a small bowl. Add a little water to loosen if necessary.

To serve, spread the tahini garlic yoghurt evenly across the bottom of a flat, round plate. Top with the roasted cauliflower and sprinkle with the herbs, almonds and dukkah. Lastly, drizzle the olive oil over.

Leftovers will keep in an airtight container in the fridge for up to 3 days.

---

**SWAP**

Cauliflower for pumpkin or give zucchini a go in the summer. Refer to Swap with the Seasons (page 12) for more ideas.

**TIP**

Try whipped feta (page 163) in place of the tahini garlic yoghurt.

**DELICIOUS WITH**

Fried Chickpea + Herb Tabbouleh (page 70) and falafel, chicken, seafood or lamb.

# Summer Vegetable One Tray Bake

Feeds: 6
Time: 35 minutes

- 1 eggplant, cut into bite-sized chunks
- 1 fennel bulb, cut into bite-sized chunks
- 2 zucchini, thinly sliced on a diagonal
- 1 red capsicum, cut into bite-sized chunks
- 1 red onion, cut into thin wedges
- 3 tablespoons cooking oil
- 1 teaspoon sea salt

- 200 g (7 oz) cherry tomatoes

- 1 cup rocket leaves
- ¼ preserved lemon, flesh and rind finely chopped
- 100 g (3½ oz) feta, crumbled
- ¼ cup pine nuts, toasted
- 2 tablespoons extra virgin olive oil

Preheat the oven to 200°C (400°F).

Place the eggplant, fennel, zucchini, capsicum and red onion on a large baking tray and toss with the cooking oil and salt. Bake for 20–25 minutes.

Add the cherry tomatoes to the baking tray, turn the oven to the grill function and cook for a further 5–8 minutes. Remove the vegetables from the oven and allow to cool slightly.

This is good served on the tray. Top the vegetables with the rocket, preserved lemon, feta and pine nuts, and olive oil on top. Gently toss everything together.

Leftovers will keep in an airtight container in the fridge for up to 3 days.

---

### SWAP

Change up the vegetables depending on what's in season. Refer to Swap with the Seasons (page 12) for ideas. You can replace the feta with smashed olives, capers or sun-dried tomatoes.

### TIP

Pine nuts are tasty but expensive. Delicious, cost-effective alternatives include almonds, pumpkin seeds and sunflower seeds.

### DELICIOUS WITH

Brown Rice, Chilli, Corn + Avocado (page 92) and chicken or seafood.

# Chilli Oil Mushrooms, Rice, Edamame + Cucumber

Feeds: 6–8
Time: 30 minutes

- 1 cup brown rice
- 2½ cups water

- 400 g (14 oz) white button mushrooms
- 2 tablespoons chilli oil, homemade or store-bought
- 1 tablespoon cooking oil
- 1 teaspoon sea salt

**Ginger Tamari Oil**

- ¼ cup extra virgin olive oil
- 2 tablespoons tamari or soy sauce
- 1 tablespoon freshly grated ginger
- 1 tablespoon apple cider vinegar
- 2 garlic cloves, crushed and finely chopped
- 2 teaspoons sesame oil
- ½ teaspoon sea salt

- ½ cucumber, cut into bite-sized chunks
- 1 cup edamame beans, blanched in boiling water for 5 minutes then drained
- 1 cup chopped coriander
- ¼ cup sesame seeds

Preheat the oven to 200°C (400°F).

Put the brown rice and water in a pot and bring to the boil. Reduce to a simmer and cook for 20-25 minutes, or until all the water has been absorbed. Remove from the heat.

Add the mushrooms to a baking tray and drizzle the chilli oil and cooking oil over them. Sprinkle with salt and toss well. Cook for 15 minutes, then remove them from the oven.

While the brown rice and mushrooms are cooking, make the ginger tamari oil. Mix all the ingredients together into a cup or small bowl.

To serve, tip the cooked brown rice into a large bowl and add 2 tablespoons of ginger tamari oil. Mix the oil through the rice with a fork. Add the mushrooms, cucumber, edamame beans, coriander and sesame seeds. Drizzle the remaining ginger tamari oil over and gently toss everything together.

Serve with a small bowl of chilli oil to drizzle on top if desired.

Leftovers will keep in an airtight container in the fridge for up to 3 days.

---

**SWAP**

Brown rice for udon or soba noodles. Mushrooms for any other vegetables such as eggplant, broccoli or zucchini. Refer to Swap with the Seasons (page 12) for more ideas.

**TIP**

Tamari is a gluten-free type of soy sauce – they can be used interchangeably if gluten is not an issue for you. You might like to double the ginger tamari oil recipe and store the excess in a jar in the fridge for up to 2 weeks. Use it to marinate chicken, prawns, tofu, beef, lamb or your favourite vegetables before roasting in the oven or grilling on the barbecue. It is also delicious drizzled over a side of salmon before baking in the oven.

**DELICIOUS WITH**

Ginger Chilli Bok Choy (page 84) and seafood or chicken.

# Mexican Beans, Charred Corn Salsa + Coriander Yoghurt

Feeds: 6
Time: 35 minutes

**Mexican Beans + Kūmara**

1 large kūmara, cut into 1 cm (½ in) slices
1 red onion, cut into thin wedges
400 g (14 oz) can black beans, drained and rinsed
2 teaspoons smoked paprika
2 teaspoons ground cumin
2 tablespoons cooking oil
1 teaspoon sea salt

½ cup millet
1 cup water

**Charred Corn Salsa**

1 tablespoon cooking oil
½ teaspoon sea salt
2 corn cobs, raw kernels cut off the cob
2 garlic cloves, crushed and finely chopped
1 avocado, cut into chunks
1 cup chopped fresh herbs
1 tablespoon extra virgin olive oil
½ teaspoon sea salt

**Coriander Yoghurt**

½ cup plain plant-based or dairy Greek yoghurt
1 cup chopped coriander
zest and juice of 1 lemon
¼ teaspoon sea salt
1-2 tablespoons water

2 cups green cabbage, thinly sliced

Preheat the oven to 200°C (400°F).

For the Mexican beans and kūmara, add everything to a baking tray and toss to combine. Bake for 25-30 minutes.

Place the millet and water in a pot and bring to the boil. Reduce to a simmer and cook for 7 minutes. Remove the pot from the heat.

For the charred corn salsa, add the cooking oil, salt, corn kernels and garlic to a frypan. Cook until the corn starts to char, then remove from the heat.

Make the coriander yoghurt by adding all the ingredients to a blender and processing until you have a smooth green yoghurt.

When the charred corn is cool, add the avocado, herbs, olive oil and salt and gently toss to combine.

To assemble the salad, place half the thinly sliced cabbage on a flat, round plate. Top this with half each of the millet, Mexican beans and kūmara and charred salsa. Lastly add half the coriander yoghurt. Repeat these layers.

Leftovers will keep in an airtight container in the fridge for up to 2 days.

---

**SWAP**

Millet for brown rice or quinoa. When corn is not in season you can use a 400 g (14 oz) can or frozen kernels instead. If you don't like coriander, use another herb or a combination such as rocket, basil, parsley and/or dill.

**TIP**

We suggest you double the coriander yoghurt recipe – it is delicious in fish tacos or dolloped over roast chicken.

**DELICIOUS WITH**

Chilli Oil Fried Green Beans (page 68) and chicken or prawns.

# Pesto Brussels Sprouts + Feta

Feeds: 6
Time: 30 minutes

- 500 g (1 lb 2 oz) Brussels sprouts, large ones cut in half
- 2 tablespoons cooking oil
- ½ teaspoon sea salt

- 2 tablespoons extra virgin olive oil
- 2 tablespoons pesto

- 50 g (2 oz) feta, crumbled
- ½ teaspoon sea salt

Preheat the oven to 200°C (400°F).

Drizzle the cooking oil over the Brussels sprouts on a baking tray. Sprinkle with the salt and toss until they are are evenly coated. Bake for 20 minutes or until golden brown and crispy.

In a small bowl or cup, mix together the olive oil and pesto.

Spoon the pesto oil over the cooked Brussels sprouts and toss gently.

To serve, transfer the Brussels sprouts to a flat, round plate or bowl. Top with the crumbled feta and sea salt.

Leftovers will keep in an airtight container in the fridge for up to 3 days.

---

### SWAP

Brussels sprouts for yams or broccoli. Refer to Swap with the Seasons (page 12) for more ideas.

### TIP

Use store-bought or homemade pesto – head to page 179 for our rocket pesto recipe. If you are dairy free, leave out the feta and sprinkle over toasted pumpkin seeds.

### DELICIOUS WITH

Turmeric Millet, Leeks + Garlic Miso Yoghurt (page 148) and chicken, salmon or red meat.

# More / Desserts

# Sticky Date Puddings + Caramel Sauce

Feeds: 6
Time: 35 minutes

**Sticky Date Puddings**

1 cup almond meal
½ cup flour
¾ cup plant-based or dairy milk
¼ cup maple syrup
⅓ cup melted coconut oil
2 teaspoons ground ginger
1 teaspoon baking soda
1 teaspoon apple cider vinegar
½ teaspoon sea salt

1 cup dates, soaked in boiling water for 5 minutes then drained

**Salted Caramel Sauce**

½ cup water
½ cup coconut sugar
¼ cup plain plant-based or dairy Greek yoghurt
1½ teaspoons cornflour
1 teaspoon sea salt

6 scoops plant-based or dairy vanilla ice-cream

Preheat the oven to 180°C (350°F).

Add all the pudding ingredients, except the dates, to a bowl and mix until well combined.

Roughly mash the dates with a fork until they create a chunky paste. Add them to the pudding mixture and mix through.

Grease a muffin tin and fill 6 holes with the pudding mixture. Bake for 20 minutes or until golden brown.

To make the salted caramel sauce, place all the ingredients in a small pot and bring to the boil. Continue to boil, stirring constantly, for 30-60 seconds to thicken. Remove from the heat.

Serve the warm puddings in individual bowls with a scoop of ice-cream and a generous amount of salted caramel sauce.

Leftover pudding and sauce will last in an airtight container in the fridge for up to 7 days.

---

**SWAP**

If you are gluten free, use buckwheat flour.

**TIP**

You can make your own almond meal by processing 1 cup almonds in your blender or food processor until a fine flour is formed. Double the salted caramel sauce recipe and store a jar in the fridge for up to 7 days. For a simple yet delicious dessert, drizzle the sauce generously over a scoop or two of your favourite vanilla ice-cream. If you are feeling even more fancy, top with salty almonds (page 213).

# Strawberry, Rhubarb + White Chocolate Crumble

Feeds: 4-6
Time: 30 minutes

6 stalks rhubarb, sliced into bite-sized pieces
2 cups strawberries, sliced lengthways
2 tablespoons cornflour
2 teaspoons coconut sugar
juice of 1 lemon
½ teaspoon sea salt

**Crumble**

1½ cups rolled oats
1 cup almond meal
⅓ cup melted coconut oil
3 tablespoons maple syrup
3 tablespoons coconut sugar
3 teaspoons ground ginger
2 teaspoons vanilla bean paste or extract
1 teaspoon baking soda
1 teaspoon sea salt
100 g (3½ oz) white chocolate, chopped

4-6 scoops plant-based or dairy vanilla ice-cream

Preheat the oven to 170°C (325°F).

Place the rhubarb and strawberries in a cast iron pan or baking dish. Add the cornflour, coconut sugar, lemon juice and salt. Toss together.

For the crumble, mix all the ingredients together in a bowl. Evenly distribute this over the rhubarb and strawberries.

Bake for 20-25 minutes. We suggest setting a timer for 10 minutes to check that the crumble isn't burning. If it is golden in colour, lay some tinfoil over the top for the rest of the cooking time.

This is best served straight out of the oven with a scoop of ice-cream.

Leftover crumble will keep in an airtight container in the fridge for up to 7 days. Alternatively you can freeze it uncooked for up to 2 months.

---

### SWAP

Use any fresh or frozen fruit, depending on what's in abundance at the time – apples, stonefruit, figs, pears, feijoas.

### TIP

To make the crumble gluten free, replace the rolled oats with ½ cup shredded coconut and ½ cup sunflower or pumpkin seeds.

### DELICIOUS WITH

Homemade or store-bought custard.

# Olive Oil Chocolate Mousse with Sea Salt

Feeds: 4-6
Time: 10 minutes

- 1 avocado
- 150 g (5½ oz) dark chocolate, melted
- ¼ cup extra virgin olive oil
- ¼ cup coconut cream
- 3 tablespoons maple syrup
- ½ teaspoon sea salt

- 4–6 tablespoons extra virgin olive oil
- 1 teaspoon sea salt

Add the avocado, melted chocolate, olive oil, coconut cream, maple syrup and salt to a blender. Process until you have a thick, smooth mousse. Pour into an airtight container and place in the fridge for at least 1 hour to set.

To serve, add a generous scoop of mousse into 6 small bowls. Create a 'well' in the middle of each and pour in 1 tablespoon extra virgin olive oil. Sprinkle with a generous pinch of salt and serve immediately.

Leftovers will keep in an airtight container in the fridge for up to 2 weeks.

---

### SWAP

Dark chocolate with milk chocolate for a less bitter mousse.

### TIP

This is a great way to use up overripe avocados. You will be blown away by how simple yet insanely decadent this dessert is. Do yourself a favour and double the recipe. If your mixture splits, an easy fix is to add 1 tablespoon of water and continue blending until the mousse becomes silky smooth again.

### DELICIOUS WITH

Roasted, stewed or preserved fruit such as stonefruit, strawberries or pears. (To roast your fruit, cut into pieces and toss in cooking oil, honey and salt. Bake at 180°C (350°F) for 10–15 minutes.) To add texture, we love topping with roasted hazelnuts.

# Blueberry + Lemon Syrup Tray Cake

Feeds: 8
Time: 40 minutes

- 1½ cups almond meal or spelt flour
- 1 cup plain plant-based or dairy Greek yoghurt
- ½ cup light flavoured olive oil or sunflower seed oil
- ½ cup fine polenta
- ½ cup coconut sugar
- 2 teaspoons baking powder
- zest and juice of 2 lemons

- 1½ cups blueberries, fresh or frozen

**Lemon Syrup**

- ¼ cup coconut sugar
- zest and juice of 2 lemons

Preheat the oven to 190°C (375°F) and line a 30 cm x 15 cm (12 in x 6 in) baking tray with baking paper.

Add all the cake ingredients except the blueberries to a bowl, and mix until well combined. Add half the blueberries and gently fold through.

Pour the cake mixture into the lined baking tray and randomly dot the remaining blueberries on top. Bake for 30 minutes.

While the cake is cooking, make the lemon syrup. Add all the ingredients to a small pot and heat until the coconut sugar has dissolved.

Remove the cake from the oven and prick it all over with a fork. Slowly pour the lemon syrup over the cake, spreading it evenly with the back of a spoon. Leave the cake to absorb the syrup for at least 15 minutes before serving.

Leftovers will keep in an airtight container in the fridge for up to 4 days.

---

**SWAP**

Coconut sugar for brown sugar. Blueberries for any fruit that is in season – we love using stonefruit, feijoas, rhubarb or pears. Chop into bite-sized pieces and fold through the cake and randomly dot on top.

**TIP**

If you don't have the right-sized baking tray, use a loaf tin or 23 cm (9 in) cake tin. Polenta makes for a delicious gluten-free cake base. It has a beautiful texture and flavour that are a perfect match for the fresh, zingy lemon.

**DELICIOUS WITH**

A dollop of plant-based or Greek yoghurt or a scoop of ice-cream.

# Raspberry Brownie Pudding

Feeds: 4
Time: 35 minutes

**Raspberry Brownie**

1 cup flour

¼ cup cacao powder

⅓ cup coconut sugar

⅓ cup melted coconut oil

½ cup plant-based or dairy milk

50 g (1¾ oz) dark chocolate, chopped

1½ teaspoons baking powder

½ teaspoon sea salt

2 cups raspberries, fresh or frozen

**Chocolate Sauce**

⅓ cup coconut sugar

3 tablespoons cacao powder

1¼ cups boiling water

½ teaspoon sea salt

4-8 scoops plant-based or dairy ice-cream

Preheat the oven to 180°C (350°F).

Mix all the brownie ingredients except the raspberries, in a bowl until well combined. Add half the raspberries and gently fold through.

Pour the brownie mixture into a baking dish and smooth the top with the back of a spoon. Lightly press the rest of the raspberries into the brownie mixture.

Whisk all the chocolate sauce ingredients together in a bowl until smooth and shiny.

Slowly pour the chocolate sauce over the uncooked brownie mixture, using the back of a large spoon to spread it right over. It will look very watery but don't panic!

Bake in the oven for 35 minutes.

To serve, spoon the raspberry brownie pudding into individual bowls and serve with a scoop or two of ice-cream.

Leftovers will keep in an airtight container in the fridge for up to 5 days.

---

**SWAP**

Raspberries for any other fresh, frozen or preserved fruit you have on hand. We love using feijoas, rhubarb, pears, stonefruit and any berries that are in abundance at the time.

**TIP**

To make this gluten free, replace the 1 cup flour with ¾ cup almond meal and ¼ cup buckwheat flour. If you don't have cacao powder, use the same amount of cocoa powder.

# Coffee Parfait, Salty Almonds + Chocolate

Feeds: 6

Time: 20 minutes + freezer time (3–4 hours)

**Coffee Parfait**

- ¾ cup coconut cream
- ⅓ cup dates, soaked in boiling water for 5 minutes then drained
- ¼ cup melted coconut oil
- ¼ cup almond butter
- 4 espresso shots
- ½ teaspoon sea salt

**Salty Almonds**

- ¾ cup almonds, roasted and chopped
- 3 tablespoons maple syrup
- 1 teaspoon sea salt

- 6 scoops plant-based or dairy vanilla ice-cream
- 50 g (2 oz) dark chocolate, chopped

Line a loaf tin with baking paper.

Add all the coffee parfait ingredients to a blender and process until smooth. Pour into the lined loaf tin and place in the freezer for 3-4 hours.

When you are ready to assemble, mix all the ingredients for the salty almonds together in a bowl.

Cut the coffee parfait into 6 even slices and arrange on 6 individual plates. Top each slice with a scoop of ice-cream, followed by a generous spoonful of salty almonds and some chopped dark chocolate. Serve immediately.

Leftovers will keep in an airtight container in the freezer for up to 2 months.

---

## SWAP

In the coffee parfait, swap the almond butter for peanut butter. For the salty almonds, change it up by swapping the almonds for any nuts and/or seeds you have in the pantry. We love using walnuts, hazelnuts or pumpkin seeds.

## TIP

If you don't like coffee, leave it out. It's just as delicious without it.

# Peanut Mousse Pie

Feeds: 8-10

Time: 25 minutes + fridge time (ideally overnight)

**Shortbread Base**

1½ cups rolled oats

½ cup almonds

½ cup dates, soaked in boiling water for 5 minutes then drained

3 tablespoons melted coconut oil

2 tablespoons peanut butter

1-2 tablespoons water

½ teaspoon sea salt

**Peanut Mousse**

300 g (10½ oz) silken tofu

1 cup peanut butter

1 cup coconut cream

⅓ cup maple syrup

1 teaspoon vanilla bean paste or extract

½ teaspoon sea salt

150 g (5½ oz) dark chocolate, chopped

½ teaspoon sea salt

Line a 23 cm (9 in) tart or cake tin with baking paper.

In a blender, process the rolled oats and almonds until you have a fine flour. Add the remaining shortbread base ingredients to the blender and process until a dough starts to form. Scrape this mixture into the lined tin and evenly press up the sides and along the base. Place in the freezer for 5-10 minutes while you make the peanut mousse.

Place all the peanut mousse ingredients in the blender and process until smooth and creamy.

Remove the shortbread base from the freezer and pour in the peanut mousse. Flatten the top with the back of a spoon or a spatula. Sprinkle the dark chocolate and salt over the top. Place in the fridge to set for at least 6 hours, ideally overnight.

Leftovers will keep in an airtight container in the fridge for up to 6 days. Alternatively you can freeze this for up to 2 months. Just allow it to sit at room temperature for at least 30 minutes to soften before eating.

---

**SWAP**

To make this gluten free, swap the rolled oats for raw buckwheat groats. Instead of using almonds in the base you can swap for pumpkin seeds, sunflower seeds or cashews.

**TIP**

Don't be put off by the tofu. It creates the most amazing creamy texture. Add 1 banana to the peanut mousse before blending to make a banoffee mousse.

**DELICIOUS WITH**

Banana slices.

# Mint + Lime Strawberries

Feeds: 4
Time: 10 minutes

250 g (9 oz) strawberries, sliced widthways

zest and juice of 1 lime

1½ tablespoons maple syrup

½ teaspoon sea salt

**Salted Coconut Crumble**

¾ cup coconut flakes

2 tablespoons maple syrup

¼ teaspoon sea salt

¼ cup chopped mint leaves

8 scoops plant-based or dairy ice-cream

Place the sliced strawberries, lime zest and juice, maple syrup and salt in a bowl and gently mix together. Allow to marinate for at least 10 minutes.

For the salted coconut crumble, heat a frypan and toast the coconut flakes for 2-3 minutes or until they begin to turn golden. Add the maple syrup and salt and cook for another 1-2 minutes. Transfer to a bowl.

To serve, gently toss the chopped mint leaves through the marinated strawberries. Add 2 scoops of ice-cream to each individual bowl. Top with the strawberries and a generous amount of salted coconut crumble. Serve immediately.

Leftover strawberries will keep in an airtight container in the fridge for up to 2 days.

---

### SWAP

Strawberries for any other berry or stonefruit. You can use a lemon instead of a lime, and honey instead of maple syrup.

### TIP

Try roasting the strawberries instead of marinating them. Preheat the oven to 180°C (350°F) and once you have mixed everything through the strawberries, arrange them on a baking tray. Roast for 10 minutes, then allow to cool slightly before serving.

### DELICIOUS WITH

A generous sprinkle of salty almonds (page 213) instead of the salted coconut crumble.

# Hazelnut Caramel Slice

Feeds: 10

Time: 40 minutes + freezer time (3 hours)

**Hazelnut Brownie**

¾ cup rolled oats

¾ cup desiccated coconut

¾ cup hazelnuts, roasted

¼ cup maple syrup

3 tablespoons cacao powder

1 tablespoon water

½ teaspoon sea salt

**Caramel**

320 g (11¼ oz) plant-based or dairy condensed milk

3 tablespoons coconut sugar

¼ teaspoon sea salt

½ cup melted coconut oil

½ cup hazelnuts, roasted

**Chocolate Layer**

150 g (5½ oz) dark chocolate, chopped

1 tablespoon hulled tahini

½ teaspoon sea salt

Line a loaf tin with baking paper.

For the brownie, add the rolled oats, coconut and hazelnuts to a blender and process just past the point of a flour. You'll know you have reached this point when you see the oily fats start to show on the side of the blender. Add the maple syrup, cacao, water and salt and blend until you have a cookie-dough consistency. Press the brownie mixture into the lined tin. Use the back of a spoon to achieve a smooth finish.

For the caramel, add the condensed milk, coconut sugar and salt to a pot and bring to the boil, stirring constantly. Once at a boil, turn down the heat to medium. Leave to simmer for 10 minutes, stirring occasionally. Finally, add the melted coconut oil and whisk until glossy and thick.

Scatter the ½ cup of whole roasted hazelnuts over the brownie base and pour the caramel on top. Evenly spread it out by gently banging the tin on the bench a couple of times. Place in the freezer for 1 hour.

After 1 hour, melt the dark chocolate in the microwave or over a double boiler. Add the tahini and salt and mix well.

Take the hazelnut caramel brownie out of the freezer and pour the chocolate layer over the top. Put it back in the freezer for 2 hours to set completely.

Cut into squares.

This will keep in an airtight container in the freezer for up to 2 months.

---

### SWAP

If you are gluten free, use raw buckwheat groats instead of rolled oats. You can use butter instead of coconut oil in the caramel if you prefer.

### TIP

Add a shot of coffee to the caramel when you add the other ingredients to the pot. The hulled tahini helps prevent the chocolate from cracking when you cut the slice into squares.

### DELICIOUS WITH

A scoop of vanilla ice-cream.

# Thank You

It really does take a village to write a cookbook.

This is our fifth book and it has taken us this long to be able to open a newly published book and instantly feel happy and proud of what we have accomplished and produced.

The journey of getting this book into your hands has been the most enjoyable one yet. Right from the beginning, *More Salad* has been everything we imagined and dreamt of, from creating the recipes right through to photography and design.

Whether this is your first Two Raw Sisters cookbook or you now have the whole collection, we hope you love this one as much as we do.

From the moment we wrote these recipes we have been making them non-stop. No matter what the occasion – dinner for one or a big family gathering – these recipes have been put under the microscope by our friends and family. You can trust us when we say they have been tried, tested and loved by many.

The main reason *More Salad* looks as good as it does is because of the team who helped us bring it all to life. A book is created by many people, not just the two of us named on the front cover. This page is therefore dedicated to acknowledging and celebrating everyone behind the scenes:

Allen & Unwin – Miff, Abba, Leonie, the team behind making this book a reality. It is always an absolute pleasure to work with this amazing group of girls. Thank you for your encouragement, guidance and advice.

Food stylist Jo Bridgford from Delivision – this is the third cookbook we have worked on together and we make a very efficient team. We had the best few weeks shooting the photos with you in Ligar Bay, memories we will treasure. Thank you for helping us bring the food and ingredients to life with your talent, care and attention to detail in every recipe we created. We are so lucky to work with you.

Incidental photographer Susannah Blatchford, the talented woman behind the lens making us look and feel our best and helping us bring the book's cover to life. We admire you for putting up with us.

Book designer Katrina Duncan and editor Rachel Scott – thank you both for your attention to detail and care. It means a lot to have people care as much as we do.

Our manager, Dean Buchanan. What a legend you are, constantly pushing us to strive for more. We couldn't do it without you.

We feel so privileged to have worked with some New Zealand brands that we have personally loved for years. Kowtow, Acme, Nicola Shuttleworth, Bryterlater – thank you for your support and collaboration. Without you, the book wouldn't look half as good as it does.

Finally, as always, we thank our family and friends for their constant support and feedback along the way.

Until next time,
Rosa & Margo x

**Want more Recipes?**

**Purchase one of our other cookbooks or download the Two Raw Sisters App below.**

# Index

## D

## T



## W



## Y



## Z